AngularJS Web Application Development Blueprints

A practical guide to developing powerful
web applications with AngularJS

Vinci Rufus

PUBLISHING

BIRMINGHAM - MUMBAI

AngularJS Web Application Development Blueprints

First published: August 2014

Production reference: 1180814

Published by Packt Publishing Ltd.
Livery Place
35 Livery Street
Birmingham B3 2PB, UK.

ISBN 978-1-78328-561-7

www.packtpub.com

Cover image by Faiz Fattohi (faizfattohi@gmail.com)

Credits

Author
Vinci Rufus

Reviewers
Jeff Cunningham
Ashutosh Das
AJ Kerrigan
Ciro Nunes
Yacine Rezgui

Commissioning Editor
Akram Hussain

Acquisition Editor
Richard Harvey

Content Development Editor
Vaibhav Pawar

Technical Editors
Shashank Desai
Menza Mathew

Copy Editors
Karuna Narayanan
Alfida Paiva
Laxmi Subramanian

Project Coordinators
Binny K. Babu
Kranti Berde

Proofreaders
Bridget Braund
Paul Hindle
Lucy Rowland

Indexers
Hemangini Bari
Mariammal Chettiyar
Rekha Nair
Priya Subramani

Graphics
Valentina D'silva

Production Coordinator
Aparna Bhagat

Cover Work
Aparna Bhagat

About the Author

Vinci Rufus has been working with frontend technologies for close to 14 years now. He started his career building games with Flash ActionScript and later moved on to JavaScript and HTML5. During his spare time, he enjoys conducting workshops and training people.

For a living, he mentors, guides, and helps grow the technology team at Razorfish Neev, primarily in the area of commerce, usability, and emerging technologies.

A sincere thanks to the awesome team at Razorfish Neev. I've learned so much working with you all.

My deepest regards to the technical reviewers, Jeff Cunningham, Ashutosh Das, AJ Kerrigan, Ciro Nunes, and Yacine Rezgui, and also to the content development editor, Vaibhav Pawar, whose insights and feedback greatly helped in adding the finishing touches for this book.

A big thank you to my family; my dad, Rufus, who learned computers only so that he could teach me; my mom, Anne, who has always encouraged me to take up challenges every time I thought it wasn't possible; my awesome kids, Shannon and Jaden, who sacrificed a lot of their play time so that I could write this book; my wife, Raina, for all the support that was instrumental in this book reaching its completion; and finally, my sister, Blaisy, who was always there to give feedback and critique my work, and with whom I could brainstorm and discuss ideas.

About the Reviewers

Jeff Cunningham is a mobile app developer at Comdata in Nashville, TN. After 15 years of working in the field of Java web development, he now enjoys the challenges of frontend and mobile development. He also reviewed the book, *AngularJS Directives, Packt Publishing*, and maintains the popular repo named AngularJS-Learning on GitHub (`https://github.com/jmcunningham/AngularJS-Learning`).

Ashutosh Das, who hails from Bangladesh, works mainly as a backend developer and his experience includes working with Django, Node.js, Laravel, and so on. He also likes to work with AngularJS. He spends his spare time writing for GitHub. He also works as a freelancer and is a part-time job holder. He is currently in the process of reviewing the book, *AngularJS UI Development, Packt Publishing*.

AJ Kerrigan is a systems analyst with a small IT department in New Jersey. His technical duties and interests include server and database administration, command-line scripting, and web development.

AngularJS Web Application Development Blueprints, Packt Publishing, represents AJ's first experience as a technical reviewer.

> I would like to thank my wife, daughter, and dog for their love, support, and endless supply of hugs. Thanks to my father as well, who provided me with my first exposure to programming (BASIC on the family TI-99/4a computer). He has been a consistent source of encouragement and guidance.

Ciro Nunes is a 22-year old frontend engineer, test-first evangelist, and specialist in large-scale architectures for heavy client-side applications. At such a young age, he has been responsible for the development of the biggest e-commerce websites from Latin America. He's also the organizer of the AngularJS SP Meetup which has more than 400 members.

Nowadays, he's working on applications for the financial market that pushes the boundaries of AngularJS.

I want to thank my family and friends for their patience, with me being so absent lately. I promise that I'm going to walk more with the dog and spend more time with you whom I love.

Yacine Rezgui is a French-Tunisian web developer. He started web developing at the age of 12, and since then, has made his passion his job. He's specialized in web development and strongly believes that it is the best cross-platform environment. He's currently the organizer of the London Phonegap Meetup.

He worked in different companies such as Médiamétrie eStat, Tequila Rapido, and GovernorHub as a freelancer.

I would like to thank my friends, James Nocentini, James Sharp, Cédric Ferretti, and Xavier Kress for supporting me on my work, my family for all their encouragement, and Xuxu for helping me to focus.

www.PacktPub.com

Support files, eBooks, discount offers, and more

You might want to visit www.PacktPub.com for support files and downloads related to your book.

Did you know that Packt offers eBook versions of every book published, with PDF and ePub files available? You can upgrade to the eBook version at www.PacktPub.com and as a print book customer, you are entitled to a discount on the eBook copy. Get in touch with us at service@packtpub.com for more details.

At www.PacktPub.com, you can also read a collection of free technical articles, sign up for a range of free newsletters and receive exclusive discounts and offers on Packt books and eBooks.

http://PacktLib.PacktPub.com

Do you need instant solutions to your IT questions? PacktLib is Packt's online digital book library. Here, you can access, read and search across Packt's entire library of books.

Why subscribe?

- Fully searchable across every book published by Packt
- Copy and paste, print and bookmark content
- On demand and accessible via web browser

Free access for Packt account holders

If you have an account with Packt at www.PacktPub.com, you can use this to access PacktLib today and view nine entirely free books. Simply use your login credentials for immediate access.

Table of Contents

Preface

The most annoying part of using any website or web application is the time we wait for pages to load. Sure, everybody is working on making the Web fast, but those 2-3 seconds that it takes for a round trip to the server does not stop you from opening multiple tabs and often forgetting which tab you originally were on.

The rapid popularity of JavaScript frameworks and technologies such as AJAX clearly show the desperate need to save those 1 or 2, second-round trips to the server, and provide the users with a more desktop-like user experience.

About JavaScript MVC frameworks

These JavaScript frameworks aren't some new revolutionary technology or a new discovery; they are all still using the same old faithful JavaScript. These JavaScript frameworks merely provide a layer of abstraction (if I may) or a more Model-View-Controller-like architecture, so that we can be more productive while building apps and don't really have to worry about mundane things.

The credit for the rising popularity of these JavaScript frameworks would go to this surge of JavaScript-based highly interactive and rich Internet applications that nowadays do so much more than just displaying data received from a backend server. All of this is possible thanks to the modern day browser and their JavaScript engines that have become faster and powerful.

There has nearly been an explosion of these JavaScript MVC frameworks, and every other day, we see a new framework being launched. While most people consider Backbone.js or SproutCore to be one of the first JavaScript frameworks, I would say Ext JS by Sencha has been among the first JavaScript frameworks and one that is still being extensively used in the corporate world mainly to build finance apps. While Backbone.js and SproutCore were launched in 2010, Version 2.0 of Ext JS was launched towards the end of 2007.

AngularJS too was launched somewhere in 2010. Around the same time, other JavaScript frameworks were sprouting up. However, it is probably the fastest growing framework in terms of user adoption, mainly due to the "wow" factor and also the backing from the big G.

Each framework has its own pros and cons, and ideally the choice of the framework would depend on the nature of your project.

> http://www.todomvc.com/ is a very nice site to understand and compare the functioning of these JavaScript frameworks.

AngularJS is currently the most popular JavaScript MVC framework. Some of the reasons for this would be as follows:

- It's among the simplest to learn
- It follows some of the best software-engineering concepts, and is ideal to build large, scalable apps
- It has a robust testing framework to run Unit tests and End-to-End tests, thus making it easy to write and run automated test cases
- It also allows for teams to work in parallel on a single application without stepping over each other's work
- It has the fastest growing community of adaptors, and the AngularJS Google Groups and IRC chats are a great place to interact with others

How AngularJS was born

AngularJS started as an internal Google project by Misko Hevery, sometime in 2009. As the story goes, Misko's team was working on a project called Google Feedback; even after six months of development and about 17,000 lines of code, they were still unhappy with the pace of development and the inability to write automated tests. That's when Misko decided to rewrite that. It took him about 3 weeks and he managed to write the whole thing in just about 1,500 lines of code.

That's when AngularJS got some serious attention internally at Google, and a team was put together to help further develop it. Around 2010, Google decided to declare it as open source under the MIT license.

The idea behind this book

The idea behind writing this book is to showcase the different types of applications that can be built on AngularJS. Besides explaining AngularJS and how to write modular and testable code, there is a fair amount of emphasis on making those apps look beautiful. So, be ready for some CSS stuff and design-related discussions.

I've tried to cover a variety of applications ranging from a simple address book, an HTML5 mobile app, an e-commerce store, a CMS framework, and also ideas on how to deploy apps on Amazon AWS.

What this book covers

This book is broken down into nine chapters.

Chapter 1, *Introduction to AngularJS and the Single Page Application*, talks about the concept of a Single Page App and how they are different from the regular web apps. We'll also learn about the basics of AngularJS by building a simple Address Book App.

Chapter 2, *Setting Up Your Rig*, talks about how having the right set of tools can be a huge productivity booster. It also makes you feel like a pro when building your AngularJS app. This chapter will talk about some of the tools such as Node.js, ExpressJS, Grunt, Yeoman, and Karma.

Chapter 3, *Rapid Prototyping with AngularJS*, talks about the ease with which one can create clickable prototypes to get a feel of how an application would look and feel before working on any backend code.

Chapter 4, *Using REST Web Services in Your AngularJS App*, will show you how to consume data from third-party REST web services using factories and the $http service.

Chapter 5, *Facebook Friends' Birthday Reminder App*, will explain directives and how we can create our Facebook login directive. We will also set up some automated tests to ensure everything is working fine.

Chapter 6, *Building an Expense Manager Mobile App*, will walk you through the process of building a responsive and touch-friendly mobile app using ngAnimate and HTML5 features such as localStorage.

Chapter 7, *Building a CMS on the MEAN Stack*, talks about how to set up an entire backend and frontend system and how AngularJS interacts with a node server and MongoDB database. We will also look at session management and interceptors.

Chapter 8, Scalable Architecture for Deployments on AWS, will teach you about AWS and its various services, and how we can deploy our app in a Server-less Architecture that can inherently scale.

Chapter 9, Building an E-Commerce Store, will show you how to directly read and write data from AWS's DynamoDB database, and upload images to S3 directly from our JavaScript app.

Appendix, AngularJS Resources. Well, you know what to expect here.

What you need for this book

You obviously don't need to read the entire book before you can start working on your first AngularJS project. I'm a firm believer of learning things the practical way, and that's why from the very first chapter, you will find yourself firing up your IDE/Text editor, and writing code and testing it on your browser.

While you will learn a couple of new features of AngularJS in each of the chapters, each chapter is still self-contained, and you can comfortably jump to any of the chapters that interest you or that you need to refer to for your project.

However, if you are just starting off with AngularJS, then I strongly recommend that you read through the first three chapters before you start jumping.

Software versions

The current stable version of AngularJS while writing this book is 1.2, and unless specified, we will be using the stable version of 1.2.17 for all the examples in this book.

You can get the latest version of AngularJS using any of the following methods:

- Download the compiled minified version from `http://www.angularjs.org`.
- Fork or clone the source code from the GitHub URL `https://github.com/angular/angular.js`.
- The recommended option for both development and production code is to call the AngularJS file directly from the Google CDN. The link to the AngularJS section on the CDN is `https://developers.google.com/speed/libraries/devguide#angularjs`.

Copying the code files

The code examples mentioned in this book can be used in your programs. However, if you choose to burn them on to CDs for redistribution or are putting up the code examples for downloads, you are required to get explicit permission from Packt Publishing.

Who this book is for

This book is mainly aimed at professionals, both designers and programmers. Thankfully, AngularJS is evolving to be a framework where both designers and programmers work together without discriminating each other as backend developers or frontend designers.

The book obviously assumes that you know your basics in HTML, CSS, and JavaScript. You understand the importance and need for writing modular, scalable, testable, and good-looking applications. You don't need to have worked with AngularJS or any other JavaScript framework to understand the topics covered. The book assumes you just met AngularJS on a blind date.

The book starts off with getting you comfortable with the basic concepts that you come across very often while working with AngularJS. We'll write some simple code just to see how AngularJS works, understanding it better, and then we'll graduate to writing cleaner and modular code.

Also, I have a chapter dedicated to setting up your development "rig" with a set of tools and plugins that will help you boost your productivity while building AngularJS apps.

Conventions

In this book, you will find a number of styles of text that distinguish between different kinds of information. Here are some examples of these styles, and an explanation of their meaning.

Code words in text, database table names, folder names, filenames, file extensions, pathnames, dummy URLs, user input, and Twitter handles are shown as follows: "Now, `angular-bootstrap` will be available for use across our application."

A block of code is set as follows:

```
<carousel interval="setInterval">
    <slide ng-repeat="slide in slides" active="slide.active">
    </slide>
</carousel>
```

When we wish to draw your attention to a particular part of a code block, the relevant lines or items are set in bold:

```
<body ng-app ng-init=" myName ='John Doe' ">
    {{myName}} is {{ 2014-1968}} years old.
    <script src=" angular.min.js " type="text/javascript "> </script>
</body>
```

Any command-line input or output is written as follows:

```
yo angular:route subscribers
```

New terms and **important words** are shown in bold. Words that you see on the screen, in menus or dialog boxes for example, appear in the text like this: "Click on the **Download** button and select the following options from the pop-up window:"

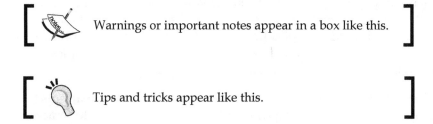

Warnings or important notes appear in a box like this.

Tips and tricks appear like this.

Reader feedback

Feedback from our readers is always welcome. Let us know what you think about this book—what you liked or may have disliked. Reader feedback is important for us to develop titles that you really get the most out of.

To send us general feedback, simply send an e-mail to feedback@packtpub.com, and mention the book title via the subject of your message.

If there is a topic that you have expertise in and you are interested in either writing or contributing to a book, see our author guide on www.packtpub.com/authors.

Customer support

Now that you are the proud owner of a Packt book, we have a number of things to help you to get the most from your purchase.

Downloading the example code

You can download the example code files for all Packt books you have purchased from your account at http://www.packtpub.com. If you purchased this book elsewhere, you can visit http://www.packtpub.com/support and register to have the files e-mailed directly to you.

Errata

Although we have taken every care to ensure the accuracy of our content, mistakes do happen. If you find a mistake in one of our books—maybe a mistake in the text or the code—we would be grateful if you would report this to us. By doing so, you can save other readers from frustration and help us improve subsequent versions of this book. If you find any errata, please report them by visiting http://www.packtpub.com/submit-errata, selecting your book, clicking on the **errata submission form** link, and entering the details of your errata. Once your errata are verified, your submission will be accepted and the errata will be uploaded on our website, or added to any list of existing errata, under the Errata section of that title. Any existing errata can be viewed by selecting your title from http://www.packtpub.com/support.

Piracy

Piracy of copyright material on the Internet is an ongoing problem across all media. At Packt, we take the protection of our copyright and licenses very seriously. If you come across any illegal copies of our works, in any form, on the Internet, please provide us with the location address or website name immediately so that we can pursue a remedy.

Please contact us at copyright@packtpub.com with a link to the suspected pirated material.

We appreciate your help in protecting our authors, and our ability to bring you valuable content.

Questions

You can contact us at questions@packtpub.com if you are having a problem with any aspect of the book, and we will do our best to address it.

1
Introduction to AngularJS and the Single Page Application

In this chapter, we'll learn what Single Page Apps are and how they differ from the regular web applications. We will also learn the fundamentals of AngularJS and go about building a simple Address Book App using it.

The list of topics to be covered in the chapter are as follows:

- What are Single Page Apps?
- Anatomy of an app
- Models and views
- Building an Address Book App
- Styling the app with CSS
- Adding items to the Address Book

Delving into Single Page Apps

Besides other things, AngularJS is primarily used to build **Single Page Apps (SPAs)**, so let us first understand its characteristics.

Single Page Apps are apps or websites wherein the entire site or app content loads within a single page. This essentially means that once the app or website is loaded in the browser, clicking on any link would not reload the entire page but would simply update certain sections within the main page itself. This gives users a very desktop-like feel while using an SPA.

Although SPAs have become very popular nowadays, the concept has been discussed as early as 2003, and the term Single Page App was coined in 2005.

Some of the technologies that play a predominant role in building SPAs are HTML, CSS, JavaScript, AJAX, and web services usually RESTful. Of these, JavaScript plays the most crucial role in building an SPA, so if you have been procrastinating on sharpening your JavaScript skills this would be the best time to get up and get started.

One of the fundamental differences in the way SPAs work against regular websites is the way the pages are built, which the user sees. Refer to the following diagram:

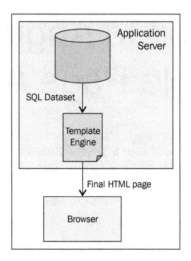

In traditional web applications that are built on the server-side technologies such as Java, PHP, and .NET, whenever a page is requested, the web server would make a request to the database, fetch the result of the query, then load the template, and dynamically generate the final page, which is sent down to the browser. As you can see here, the web server is doing all the heavy lifting, and as the traffic to the server increases, the web server becomes a bottleneck. This is why popular high-traffic sites need a lot of servers.

Single Page Apps, especially those built on JavaScript frameworks such as AngularJS work in a slightly different fashion. Refer to the following diagram:

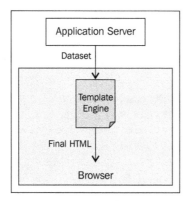

In an SPA architecture, the entire template along with the HTML, JavaScript, and CSS is downloaded to the user's browser, so when a request is made, content is sent from the web server and the page is built on the client side on the user's browser. Here, the browser is doing the heavy lifting. In such an architecture, the web server is merely passing raw data and is not involved in building the pages. The pages are built on each user's browser and hence even if the traffic to the site increases, the server doesn't get overloaded, as it would have in a regular web app architecture.

Another thing that makes SPAs wonderful is that the presentation layer can be completely decoupled from the backend layer.

Anatomy of a simple AngularJS app

Perform the following steps:

1. To start, let's first download a version of AngularJS from `http:www.angularjs.org`.

2. Click on the **Download** button and select the following options from the pop-up window:
    - **Branch**: Select **Stable**
    - **Build**: Select **Minified**

3. Download the JS file and place it in your project's folder.

Let us start by writing a simple AngularJS app. Create an `index.html` file with the following code:

```
<!DOCTYPE html>
<html>
<head>
    <title>AngularJS Basic</title>
</head>

<body ng-app ng-init=" myName ='John Doe' ">
    {{myName}} is {{ 2014-1968}} years old.
    <script src=" angular.min.js " type="text/javascript "> </script>
    </body>
</html>
```

This is a regular HTML page with the HTML5 `doctype` and the AngularJS JavaScript file being called in. Now, let us look at specific syntaxes of AngularJS and what they mean. The syntaxes are as follows:

- `ng-app`: This defines the element within which AngularJS will bootstrap itself. In most cases, we would add it to the `<html>` or `<body>` tag. It is also possible you would be building a regular application in Java, PHP, or .NET and only a section of it would be running an AngularJS app, in such cases you would add `ng-app` to the `<div>` tag wrapping the app component.

- `ng-init`: This is used to define the initialization tasks. In this example, we are creating a model called `myName` with the value `John Doe`.

 Using `ng-init` is not recommended for production apps. As we will see later in this chapter, the ideal way to initialize the variable would be in the controller instead of directly writing it in the view.

- `{{ }}`: The double curly brackets are used to output the data stored in models. In this case, `{{myName}}` outputs the value `John Doe`. These curly brackets can also be used for expressions, as in the example `{{2014-1968}}` outputs the result `46`. This is very similar to how other templating engines such as Mustache or Smarty work.

- **Directives**: The `ng-app` and the `ng-init` tags that you see in the preceding sample code are called **Directives**. They are an integral part of any AngularJS app and it is through these directives that AngularJS is able to modify the DOM element of an application. AngularJS comes with a whole set of predefined directives many of which we will use as we go through this book. The good thing about AngularJS is that you can also create your own custom directives that can meet your specific requirements.

Models and views

In AngularJS, a model could be a primitive, a hash table, or a JavaScript object. The data from the model can be displayed in the view using the {{ }} expression.

Models can be defined in multiple ways. Like we saw in the first example, we can define the model within the ng-init directive. It can be created in the template within the expression as follows:

```
<button ng-click="firstName='John Doe' ">click </button>
```

Alternatively, it could also be created within a controller using the scope, which is the ideal way to do it. Refer to the following code:

```
<!DOCTYPE html>
<html ng-app>
<head>
    <title>Model in Scope</title>
</head>
<body ng-controller="PeopleController">
    {{person.name}} lives in {{person.city}}
    <script src="angular.min.js" type="text/javascript"></script>
    <script type="text/javascript">
    function PeopleController($scope) {
        $scope.person = {
            name: "John Doe",
            city: "New York"
        }
    }
    </script>
</body>
</html>
```

In the preceding example, we created a controller called PeopleController and defined the model person, which is storing the data as a hash table. The $scope is an AngularJS object that is able to reference the JavaScript object model as a property.

Building an Address Book App

In the earlier examples, we saw the different ways of creating models. When creating production grade or large-scale applications, which involve graphical interfaces, it is compulsory to follow the **Model View Controller (MVC)** design pattern.

Building on the previous code example, we'll go ahead and build a simple Address Book App.

Let's start by creating our models in a controller called `PeopleController`. We'll now write all our JavaScripts in a file called `scripts.js`. Your `scripts.js` file should look like this:

```
function PeopleController($scope){
$scope.people=[
    {name:"John Doe", phone: "3452345678", city:"New York"},
    {name:"Sarah Parker", phone: "1236548769", city:"Chicago"},
    {name:"Little John", phone: "4567853432", city:"Los Angeles"},
    {name:"Adam Doe", phone: "9025673152", city:"Las Vegas"}
        ];
}
```

Here we are defining the controller called `PeopleController` and creating our model called `people`. The model contains three attributes: `name`, `phone`, and `city`.

Now, let us get our markup in place. Let us call the file `index.html` using the following code:

```
<!DOCTYPE html>
<html ng-app>
    <head>
            <title>Address Book</title>
    </head>
    <body ng-controller="PeopleController">
    <h1>Address Book</h1>
    <div>
            <div ng-repeat="person in people">
                    <div>{{person.name}} - {{person.phone}}</div>
                    <span>{{person.city}} </span>
            </div>
    </div>
    <script src= "angular.min.js" type="text/javascript"></script>
    <script src= "scripts.js" type="text/javascript"></script>
    </body>
</html>
```

> It is always a good practice to load your JS files at the end of the page just above the body tag and not in the head. You can read more about why this matters here at `https://developer.yahoo.com/performance/rules.html`.

As you can see here, we are defining the HTML5 `doctype` in the first line, and then we initialize the AngularJS application by using the `ng-app` directive. You'll also notice that we are using the `ng-controller` directive and assigning `PeopleController` to it. By doing so, we are defining the section of the DOM that is now within the scope of this controller.

You'll also notice a new directive called `ng-repeat`; this is the built-in directive used to display a list of items from a collection. The `ng-repeat` directive would simply duplicate the DOM element and bind the defined properties of the data object.

As you can see, `ng-repeat` makes it so easy and clean to display record sets as compared to doing this in jQuery or plain vanilla JavaScript.

Now, run your `index.html` in the browser and you should be seeing the names with their phone numbers and cities being displayed. The data from our model is showing up, which is good. Let us also inspect the code to have a look at the changes AngularJS is making to our markup.

All modern browsers allow you to inspect the source. And in most cases you can simply right-click on the page and select **Inspect Element**. In case you are not comfortable with **Inspect**, you can also do **View Source**. Refer to the following screenshot:

By the way, here I'm using Firebug, an awesome add-on for Mozilla Firefox.

As you look through the code, you'll notice that AngularJS is making a fair bit of change to the markup.

The first thing you'll notice is that AngularJS adds a class called `ng-scope` to every DOM element where the scope is initialized (we will get to what a scope is, in just a bit). It duplicates the entire DOM present within the `ng-repeat` directive. It is also adding a class called `ng-binding` to every element where the data is bound.

AngularJS will add different CSS classes depending on the directive being used. These can come in handy when you want to style, for example, the validation messages while working with forms. We'll see more about this in the chapters ahead.

Understanding the scope in AngularJS

Let us now look at this thing called the **scope**. As you might have noticed, we defined our people controller with a `$scope` parameter. We also had to define our people model as a part of this scope. While inspecting the elements, we also noticed multiple `ng-scope` classes being defined. So, what exactly is this scope and is it really that important?

As per AngularJS's documents, the scope object refers to the application model and provides an execution context for the expressions in the views.

The expression `{{person.name}}` is able to display the content only because the name is a property that can be accessed by the scope.

Another important thing to note is that every AngularJS app will have a root scope created at the `ng-app` directive. Many other directives could also create their own scope. Scopes are arranged in a hierarchical fashion following the DOM structure of the page. Child Scopes prototypically inherit from their parent scope.

The exception to this is in cases where a directive uses a scope option, it creates an isolated scope. More information about the directives and isolated scope is available in *Chapter 5, Facebook Friends' Birthday Reminder App*.

We'll get a better understanding of it as we see other examples.

Styling the app

Now, let us style the application to make it look a little better. We'll go back to our index.html and add a few CSS classes as follows:

```html
<!DOCTYPE html>
<html ng-app>
    <head>
            <title>Address Book</title>
<link rel="stylesheet" type="text/css" href="styles.css">
    </head>
    <body ng-controller="PeopleController">
        <h1>Address Book</h1>
    <div class="wrapper">
            <div class="contact-item" ng-repeat="person in people">
                <div class="name">{{person.name}} - {{person.phone}}</
div>
                <div class="city">{{person.city}} </div>

            </div>
    </div>

    <script src= "angular.min.js" type="text/javascript"></script>
    <script src= "scripts.js" type="text/javascript"></script>
    </body>
</html>
```

Now let's create our styles.css with the following CSS styling:

```css
body{
    font-family: sans-serif;
    font-weight: 100;
    background:#ccc;
}
h1{
    text-align: center;
    color:#666;
    text-shadow:0px 2px 0px #fff;

}

.name{
    font-size:18px;
}
```

```css
.city{
    font-style: italic;
    font-size: 13px;
}

.wrapper{
    width:550px;
    margin: 0 auto;
    box-shadow:5px 5px 5px #555;
    background: #fff;
    border-radius: 15px;
    padding: 10px;

}
.contact-item{
    border-bottom: thin solid #ccc;
    padding:10px;
}
```

As you can see from the CSS styles, we first style the body to give it a light gray background color using the #ccc (#ccc is the short code for #cccccc) hex code.

The H1 heading tag is styled to align center, with a dark gray text color and a text shadow. The styling for .name and .city is straightforward. Now, let us look at the styles for .wrapper using the following code:

```css
.wrapper{
    width:650px;
    margin: 0 auto;
    box-shadow:5px 5px 5px #555;
    background: #fff;
    border-radius: 15px;
    padding: 10px;

}
```

Here, we are setting width of the div to 650px. The margin with 0 auto is used to place the div to the center of the screen irrespective of the screen resolution.

Downloading the example code

You can download the example code files for all Packt books you have purchased from your account at http://www.packtpub.com. If you purchased this book elsewhere, you can visit http://www.packtpub.com/support and register to have the files e-mailed directly to you.

Now to make it look a little better, we'll give it a box-shadow and border radius. The following diagram explains what the options of the border radius mean:

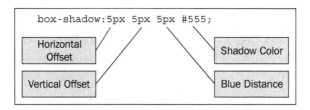

For the `.contact-item` list, we give a border-bottom and some padding so that things stay a little spaced out.

With all this CSS in place, your app should be looking like this:

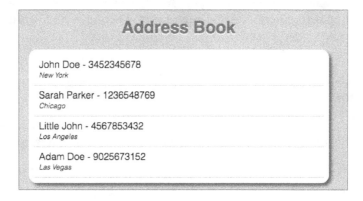

Sorting the contacts alphabetically

This looks nice, but it would be a good idea to have the names sorted alphabetically. For this, we will use AngularJS's built-in filter called `orderBy`.

In AngularJS, filters are used to format the data. One can use AngularJS's predefined filters or create your own. We'll learn more about filters later in this book.

All we need to do is modify the following section of the `index.html` as follows:

```
<div class="contact-item" ng-repeat="person in people|
orderBy:'name'">
<div class="name">{{person.name}} - {{person.phone}}</div>
<span class="city">{{person.city}} </span>
</div>
```

Refresh your Index.html in the browser and you should notice the names are now sorted alphabetically.

Adding contacts to the Address Book

Now that we have our Address Book displaying our contacts nicely, let's now create a form to add contacts.

Let us add the markup for the Add a Contact form in the index.html file within the body tag as follows:

```html
<div class="wrapper">
    <h2>Add a Contact</h2>
    Name: <input type="text" ng-model="newPerson.name"></input>
    Phone: <input type="text" ng-model="newPerson.phone"></input>
    City: <input type="text" ng-model="newPerson.city"></input>
        <button ng-click="Save()">Save</button>
</div>
```

The preceding code is rather straightforward. We create a new div and reuse the wrapper class to style it.

We are adding the three textboxes for the name, phone, and city attributes. We bind these three textboxes to a model object called newPerson as follows:

- ng-model='newPerson.name'
- ng-model='newPerson.phone'
- ng-model='newPerson.city'

We are also adding a button called **Save** and using the ng-click directive that will call the Save() function when the button is clicked.

Now, let us look at the JavaScript code that we will be writing in our scripts.js file:

```javascript
$scope.Save=function(){
$scope.people.push({name:$scope.newPerson.name, phone:$scope.
newPerson.phone, city:$scope.newPerson.city});
}
```

> Since the Save() function is accessing the scope within the PeopleController function, it is imperative that the Save() function is written within the PeopleController function in the scripts.js file.

In the $scope.Save function, we simply capture the values from the input boxes and push this into our main people model.

Let us now refresh our index.html and try it out. Fill up the form and save it and you will immediately see it get added to the Address Book. This happens thanks to one of the many cool features of AngularJS called two-way data binding.

The ng-show and ng-hide directives

While the app is good as it is, maybe it's a good idea to have a button called **Add Contact** and display the **Add Contact** form only when that button is clicked.

Let us make use of AngularJS's ng-show and ng-hide directives to control the visibility of our **Add Contact** form.

The way they work is very straightforward. If the attribute ng-show='true', then the div is visible and vice versa. A point to note is that ng-show and ng-hide merely control the visibility of the DOM element.

Let's add our button called **Add Contact** and set up the ng-show and ng-hide directives such that when you click on **Add Contact**, the form shows up and at the same time this button disappears. And when the **Save** button is clicked, the form is hidden and the **Add Contact** button shows up again.

Let's modify our index.html as follows:

```
<center><button ng-click="ShowForm()" ng-hide="formVisibility "> Add
Contact</button></center>
    <div ng-show="formVisibility " class="wrapper">
          <h2>Add a Contact</h2>
    Name: <input type="text" ng-model="newPerson.name"></input>
    Phone: <input type="text" ng-model="newPerson.phone"></input>
    City: <input type="text" ng-model="newPerson.city"></input>
          <button ng-click="Save()">Save</button>
    </div>
```

We set the button to ng-hide='formVisibility' because when the value of formVisibility becomes true, it will hide the button. Similarly, ng-show= formVisibility will make the **Add Contact** form display when the value of formVisibility is true.

Now, let's add the piece of JavaScript to set the formVisibility values. Add the following code to your scripts.js file as follows:

```
$scope.ShowForm=function(){
$scope.formVisibility=true;
}
```

Make sure this new function is written within the main `PeopleController` function.

We will also add one line in our existing `$scope.Save` function to set the value of `formVisibility` to `false`.

Please update the `$scope.Save()` function as highlighted in the following code:

```
$scope.Save = function() {

    $scope.people.push({
        name: $scope.newPerson.name,
        phone: $scope.newPerson.phone,
        city: $scope.newPerson.city
    });
    $scope.formVisibility = false;

}
```

Reload your `index.html` and see the buttons in action.

Oh and just because we don't like the way those default buttons look, lets add a little bit of style to it.

Add the following CSS classes to your `styles.css` file:

```
button
{
    background:#080;
    color:#fff;
    padding:5px 15px;
    border-radius: 5px;
    border: thin solid #060;
"margin: 5px auto;"
}
button:hover{
    background: #0A0;
}
```

What we are simply doing here is setting a dark green color background for the button, giving the text a white color, and giving it some padding five pixels from the top- and bottom-side and 15 pixels from the left-hand side and right-hand side and adding some border radius.

The button:hover is a light green background color just to show the highlight when the user hovers the cursor over the button.

Reload your index.html page and we have our very first working and reasonably good-looking Address Book Application.

Summary

This concludes our first chapter. To quickly summarize, we went about building our Address Book App and in doing so learned about the various AngularJS directives such as ng-app and ng-repeat. We saw how two-way data bindings and expressions work and the importance of scope. We also saw how we can hide and show certain elements using the ng-show and ng-hide directives. Last but not least, we used some simple and easy CSS3 features to style our app.

In the next chapter, we will see the various tools that frontend developers should ideally have in their toolbox and how to go about using them.

2
Setting Up Your Rig

I'm sure you would have heard the saying, "A tool man is known by the tools he keeps." OK fine, I just made that up, but that's actually true, especially when it comes to programming. Sure you can build complete and fully functional AngularJS apps just using a simple text editor and a browser, but if you want to work like a ninja, then make sure that you start using some of these tools as a part of your development workflow.

Do note that these tools are not mandatory to build AngularJS apps. Their use is recommended mainly to help improve the productivity.

In this chapter, we will see how to set up and use the following productivity tools:

- Node.js
- Grunt
- Yeoman
- Karma
- Protractor

Since most of us are running a Mac, Windows, Ubuntu, or another flavor of the Linux operating system, we'll be covering the deployment steps common for all of them.

Setting up Node.js

Depending on your technology stack, I strongly recommend you have either Ruby or Node.js installed.

In case of AngularJS, most of the productivity tools or plugins are available as **Node Package Manager (npm)**, and, hence, we will be setting up Node.js along with npm. Node.js is an open source JavaScript-based platform that uses an event-based Input/output model, making it lightweight and fast.

Let us head over to www.nodejs.org and install Node.js. Choose the right version as per your operating system.

The current version of Node.js at the time of writing this book is v0.10.x which comes with npm built in, making it a breeze to set up Node.js and npm.

 Node.js doesn't come with a **Graphical User Interface (GUI)**, so to use Node.js, you will need to open up your terminal and start firing some commands. Now would also be a good time to brush up on your DOS and Unix/Linux commands.

After installing Node.js, the first thing you'd want to check is to see if Node.js has been installed correctly.

So, let us open up the terminal and write the following command:

```
node --version
```

This should output the version number of Node.js that's installed on your system. The next would be to see what version of npm we have installed. The command for that would be as follows:

```
npm --version
```

This will tell you the version number for your npm.

Creating a simple Node.js web server with ExpressJS

For basic, simple AngularJS apps, you don't really need a web server. You can simply open the HTML files from your filesystem and they would work just fine. However, as you start building complex applications where you are passing data in JSON, web services, or using a **Content Delivery Network (CDN)**, you would find the need to use a web server.

The good thing about AngularJS apps is that they could work within any web server, so if you already have IIS, Apache, Nginx, or any other web server running on your development environment, you can simply run your AngularJS project from within the web root folder.

In case you don't have a web server and are looking for a lightweight web server, then let us set one up using Node.js and ExpressJS.

One could write the entire web server in pure Node.js; however, ExpressJS provides a nice layer of abstraction on top of Node.js so that you can just work with the ExpressJS APIs and don't have to worry about the low-level calls.

So, let's first install the ExpressJS module for Node.js.

Open up your terminal and fire the following command:

```
npm install -g express-generator
```

This will globally install ExpressJS. Omit the -g to install ExpressJS locally in the current folder.

When installing ExpressJS globally on Linux or Mac, you will need to run it via sudo as follows:

```
sudo npm install -g express-generator
```

This will let npm have the necessary permissions to write to the protected local folder under the user. The next step is to create an ExpressJS app; let us call it my-server. Type the following command in the terminal and hit enter:

```
express my-server
```

You'll see something like this:

```
create : my-server
   create : my-server/package.json
   create : my-server/app.js
   create : my-server/public
   create : my-server/public/javascripts
   create : my-server/public/images
   create : my-server/public/stylesheets
   create : my-server/public/stylesheets/style.css
   create : my-server/routes
   create : my-server/routes/index.js
   create : my-server/routes/user.js
   create : my-server/views
   create : my-server/views/layout.jade
   create : my-server/views/index.jade

   install dependencies:
     $ cd my-server && npm install

   run the app:
     $ DEBUG=my-server ./bin/www
```

This will create a folder called `my-server` and put in a bunch of files inside the folder.

 The `package.json` file is created, which contains the skeleton of your app. Open it and ensure the name says `my-server`; also, note the dependencies listed.

Now, to install ExpressJS along with the dependencies, first change into the `my-server` directory and run the following command in the terminal:

```
cd my-server
npm install
```

Now, in the terminal, type in the following command:

```
npm start
```

Open your browser and type `http://localhost:3000` in the address bar. You'll get a nice ExpressJS welcome message. Now to test our Address Book App created in *Chapter 1, Introduction to AngularJS and the Single Page Application*, we will copy our `index.html`, `scripts.js`, and `styles.css` into the `public` folder located within `my-server`.

 I'm not copying the `angular.js` file because we'll use the CDN version of the AngularJS library.

Open up the `index.html` file and replace the following code:

```
<script src= "angular.min.js" type="text/javascript"> </script>
```

With the CDN version of AngularJS as follows:

```
<script src="//ajax.googleapis.com/ajax/libs/angularjs/1.2.17/angular.
min.js"></script>
```

A question might arise, as to what if the CDN is unreachable. In such cases, we can add a fall back to use a local version of the AngularJS library.

We do this by adding the following script after the CDN link is called:

```
<script>window.angular || document.write('<script src="lib/angular/
angular.min.js"><\/script>');</script>
```

Save the file in the browser and enter `localhost:3000/index.html`. Your Address Book is now running from a server and taking advantage of Google's CDN to serve the AngularJS file.

Referencing the files using only // is also called the protocol independent absolute path. This means that the files are requested using the same protocol that is being used to call the parent page. For example, if the page you are loading is via https://, then the CDN link will also be called via HTTPS.

This also means that when using // instead of http:// during development, you will need to run your app from within a server instead of a filesystem.

Setting up Grunt

Grunt is a JavaScript-based task runner. It is primarily used for automating tasks such as running unit tests, concatenating, merging, and minifying JS and CSS files. You can also run shell commands. This makes it super easy to perform server cleanups and deploy code. Essentially, Grunt is to JavaScript what Rake would be to Ruby or Ant/Maven would be to Java.

Installing Grunt-cli

Installing Grunt-cli is slightly different from installing other Node.js modules. We first need to install the Grunt's **Command Line Interface (CLI)** by firing the following command in the terminal:

```
npm install -g grunt-cli
```

Mac or Linux users can also directly run the following command:

```
sudo npm install -g grunt-cli
```

Make sure you have administrative privileges. Use sudo if you are on a Mac or Linux system. If you are on Windows, right-click and open the command prompt with administrative rights. An important thing to note is that installing Grunt-cli doesn't automatically install Grunt and its dependencies.

Grunt-cli merely invokes the version of Grunt installed along with the Grunt file. While this may seem a little complicated at start, the reason it works this way is so that we can run different versions of Grunt from the same machine. This comes in handy when your project has dependencies on a specific version of Grunt.

Creating the package.json file

To install Grunt first, let's create a folder called `my-project` and create a file called `package.json` with the following content:

```
{
  "name": "My-Project",
  "version": "0.1.0",
  "devDependencies": {
    "grunt": "~0.4.5",
    "grunt-contrib-jshint": "~0.10.0",
    "grunt-contrib-concat": "~0.4.0",
    "grunt-contrib-uglify": "~0.5.0",
  "grunt-shell": "~0.7.0"

  }
}
```

Save the file. The `package.json` is where you define the various parameters of your app; for example, the name of your app, the version number, and the list of dependencies needed for the app.

Here we are calling our app `My-Project` with Version 0.1.0, and listing out the following dependencies that need to be installed as a part of this app:

- `grunt` (v0.4.5): This is the main Grunt application
- `grunt-contrib-jshint` (v0.10.0): This is used for code analysis
- `grunt-contrib-concat` (v0.4.0): This is used to merge two or more files into one
- `grunt-contrib-uglify` (v0.5.0): This is used to minify the JS file
- `grunt-shell` (v0.7.0): This is the Grunt shell used for running shell commands

Visit `http://gruntjs.com/plugins` to get a list of all the plugins available for Grunt and also their exact names and version numbers.

> You may also choose to create a default `package.json` file by running the following command and answering the questions:
>
> **npm init**
>
> Open the `package.json` file and add the dependencies as mentioned earlier.

Now that we have the `package.json` file, load the terminal and navigate into the `my-project` folder. To install Grunt and the modules specified in the file, type in the following command:

```
npm install --save-dev
```

You'll see a series of lines getting printed in the console, let that continue for a while and wait until it returns to the command prompt. Ensure that the last line printed by the previous command ends with `OK code 0`.

Once Grunt is installed, a quick version check command will ensure that Grunt is installed. The command is as follows:

```
grunt --version
```

There is a possibility that you got a bunch of errors and it ended with a **not ok code 0** message. There could be multiple reasons why that would have happened, ranging from errors in your code to a network connection issue or something changing at Grunt's end due to a new version update.

If `grunt --version` throws up an error, it means Grunt wasn't installed properly. To reinstall Grunt, enter the following commands in the terminal:

```
rm -rf node_modules
npm cache clean
npm install
```

Windows users may manually delete the `node_modules` folder from Windows Explorer, before running the cache clean command in the command prompt.

 Refer to `http://www.gruntjs.com` to troubleshoot the problem.

Creating your Grunt tasks

To run our Grunt tasks, we'll need a JavaScript file. So, let's copy our `scritps.js` from the previous chapter and place it into the `my-projects` folder.

The next step is to create a Grunt file that will list out the tasks that we need Grunt to perform.

For now, we will ask it to do four simple tasks, first check if our JS code is clean using JSHint, then we will merge three JS files into one and then minify the JS file, and finally we will run some shell commands to clean up.

Until Version 0.3, the init command was a part of the Grunt tool and one could create a blank project using grunt-init. With Version 0.4, init is now available as a separate tool called grunt-init and needs to be installed using the npm install -g grunt-init command line. Also note that the structure of the grunt.js file from Version 0.4 onwards is fairly different from the earlier versions you've used.

For now, we will resort to creating the Grunt file manually. Refer to the following screenshot:

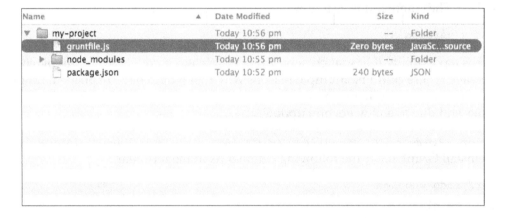

In the same location as where you have your package.json, create a file called gruntfile.js as shown earlier and type in the following code:

```
module.exports = function(grunt) {
    // Project configuration.
    grunt.initConfig({

jshint:{
    all:['scripts.js']
}
    });

    grunt.loadNpmTasks('grunt-contrib-jshint');
// Default task.
grunt.registerTask('default', ['jshint']);
};
```

To start, we will add only one task which is `jshint` and specify `scripts.js` in the list of files that need to be linted. In the next line, we specify `grunt-contrib-jshint` as the `npm` task that needs to be loaded. In the last line, we define the `jshint` as the task to be run when Grunt is running in default mode. Save the file and in the terminal run the following command:

`grunt`

You would probably get to see the following message in the terminal:

```
Running "jshint:all" (jshint) task
Linting scripts.js ...ERROR
[L18:C2] W033: Missing semicolon.
}
Linting scripts.js ...ERROR
[L24:C2] W033: Missing semicolon.
}

Warning: Task "jshint:all" failed. Use --force to continue.
```

So JSHint is saying that we are missing a semicolon on lines 18 and 24. Oh! Did I mention that JSHint is like your very strict math teacher from high school.

Let's open up `scripts.js` and put in those semicolons and rerun Grunt. Now you should get a message in green saying **1 file lint free. Done without errors**.

Let's add some more tasks to Grunt. We'll now ask it to concatenate and minify a couple of JS files. Since we currently have just one file, let's go and create two dummy JS files called `scripts1.js` and `scripts2.js`.

In `scripts1.js` we'll simply write an empty function as follows:

```
// This is from script 1
function Script1Function(){
    //------//
}
```

Similarly, in `scripts2.js` we'll write the following:

```
// This is from script 2
function Script2Function(){
    //------//
}
```

Save these files in the same folder where you have `scripts.js`.

Grunt tasks to merge and concatenate files

Now, let's open our Grunt file and add the code for both the tasks—to merge the JS file, and minify them as follows:

```
module.exports = function(grunt) {

    // Project configuration.
    grunt.initConfig({

jshint:{
    all:['scripts.js']
},

concat: {
  dist: {
      src: ['scripts.js', 'scripts1.js','scripts2.js'],
      dest: 'merged.js'
          }
      },

uglify: {
    dist: {
    src: 'merged.js',
    dest: 'build/merged.min.js'
            }
        }
    });

grunt.loadNpmTasks('grunt-contrib-jshint');
grunt.loadNpmTasks('grunt-contrib-concat');
grunt.loadNpmTasks('grunt-contrib-uglify');

// Default task.
grunt.registerTask('default', ['jshint','concat','uglify']);

};
```

As you can see from the preceding code, after the jshint task, we added the concat task. Under the src attribute, we define the files separated by a comma that need to be concatenated. And in the dest attribute, we specify the name of the merged JS file.

It is very important that the files are entered in the same sequence as they need to be merged. If the sequence of the files entered is incorrect, the merged JS file will cause errors in your app.

The `uglify` task is used to minify the JS file and the structure is very similar to the `concat` task. We add the `merged.js` file to the `src` attribute and in the `dest` attribute, we will place the `merged.min.js` file into a folder called `build`.

 Grunt will auto create the `build` folder.

After defining the tasks, we will load the necessary plugins, namely the `grunt-contrib-concat` and the `grunt-contrib-uglify`, and finally we will register the `concat` and `uglify` tasks to the `default` task.

Save the file and run Grunt. And if all goes well, you should see Grunt running these tasks and informing the status of each of the tasks.

If you get the final message saying, **Done, without any errors**, it means things went well, and this was your lucky day!

If you now open your `my-project` folder in the file manager, you should see a new file called `merged.js`. Open it in the text editor and you'll notice that all the three files have been merged into this. Also, go into the `build/merged.min.js` file and verify whether the file is minified.

Running shell commands via Grunt

Another really helpful plugin in Grunt is `grunt-shell`. This allows us to effectively run clean-up activities such as deleting `.tmp` files and moving files from one folder to another.

Let's see how to add the shell tasks to our Grunt file. Add the following highlighted piece of code to your Grunt file:

```
module.exports = function(grunt) {

    // Project configuration.
    grunt.initConfig({

jshint:{
    all:['scripts.js']
},
```

```
    concat: {
        dist: {
            src: ['scripts.js', 'scripts1.js','scripts2.js'],
            dest: 'merged.js'
                }
            },
    uglify: {
        dist: {
        src: 'merged.js',
        dest: 'build/merged.min.js'
                }
            } ,
    shell: {
        multiple: {
            command: [
                'rm -rf merged.js',
                'mkdir deploy',
                'mv build/merged.min.js deploy/merged.min.js'
            ].join('&&')
        }
    }
        });

    grunt.loadNpmTasks('grunt-contrib-jshint');
    grunt.loadNpmTasks('grunt-contrib-concat');
    grunt.loadNpmTasks('grunt-contrib-uglify');
    grunt.loadNpmTasks('grunt-shell');

    // Default task.
    grunt.registerTask('default', ['jshint','concat','uglify','shell']);

    };
```

As you can see from the code we added, we are first deleting the merged.js file, then creating a new folder called deploy and moving our merged.min.js file into it. Windows users would need to use the appropriate DOS commands for deleting and copying the files.

Note that .join('&&') is used when you want Grunt to run multiple shell commands. The next steps are to load the npm tasks and add shell to the default task list. To see Grunt perform all these tasks, run the Grunt command in the terminal.

Once it's done, open up the filesystem and verify whether Grunt has done what you had asked it to do. Just like we used the preceding four plugins, there are numerous other plugins that you can use with Grunt to automate your tasks.

A point to note is while the default Grunt command will run all the tasks mentioned in the `grunt.registerTask` statement, if you would need to run a specific task instead of all of them, then you can simply type the following in the command line:

```
grunt jshint
```

Alternatively, you can type the following command:

```
grunt concat
```

Alternatively, you can type the following command:

```
grunt ugligy
```

At times if you'd like to run just two of the three tasks, then you can register them separately as another bundled task in the Grunt file. Open up the `gruntfile.js` file, and just after the line where you have registered the default task, add the following code:

```
grunt.registerTask('concat-min', ['concat','uglify']);
```

This will register a new task called `concat-min` and will run only the `concat` and `uglify` tasks.

In the terminal run the following command:

```
grunt concat-min
```

Verify whether Grunt only concatenated and minified the file and didn't run JSHint or your shell commands.

> You can run `grunt --help` to see a list of all the tasks available in your Grunt file.

Yeoman – the workflow tool

Yeoman prefers to be known as a workflow rather than just a tool. It is actually a collection of three tools that help you manage your workflow efficiently. The tools that come as a part of Yeoman are as follows:

- **Yo**: This is a scaffolding tool and using the numerous generators available, one can quickly create the skeleton of your project. Yo has a generator to build AngularJS apps and we will be using that later in this chapter.

- **Grunt**: This is used to run the tasks that will help you preview, test, and build the app.
- **Bower**: This is an ideal tool for dependency management. Yeoman uses it to automatically search and download the necessary scripts.

Let's go about installing Yeoman and playing around with it a bit.

Installing Yeoman

To install Yeoman, make sure you are running it with administrative privileges. Enter the following command in the terminal:

```
sudo npm install -g yo
```

Next, let's install the AngularJS generator using the following command:

```
sudo npm install - g generator-angular
```

Now, let's create our project directory and create the skeleton for our project. We will call our app Yoho; so, first let's create a folder called yoho. Enter the following command in the terminal:

```
mkdir yoho
cd yoho
yo angular
```

It's now going to start asking a series of questions, answer Y for all except the question, "Would you like to use Sass (with Compass)?". Answer N for this one.

 The reason we say no here is because for now we will use vanilla CSS. Using Saas and Compass is however strongly recommended while building large applications.

Once `yo-angular` has finished doing whatever it had to do, go into your `yoho` folder and you'll notice a whole bunch of files and folders, as shown in the following screenshot:

Yeoman has created the skeleton of your AngularJS app along with everything you will need for this project.

Before we go into the details of the different files, one thing to note is that your `node_modules` folder is empty. This means Yeoman has only created the `package.json` file with all `devdependencies` listed out, but hasn't downloaded them yet.

We will need to run the following command:

```
npm install
```

This will download and install all the dependencies listed out in the `package.json` file. Once it's finished installing, verify that the `node_modules` folder now has folders such as `grunt-contrib-clean` and `grunt-contrib-concat` within it.

Ok, now, let's try and make sense of all the files that Yeoman has created. Refer to the following table:

Filename	Description
`app/404.html`	This is the 404 error page that will show up, when the user types in a wrong URL or the Angular app couldn't find the page mentioned in the URL.
`app/favicon.ico`	This is the icon that will show up in the browser tab of your app. Make sure you replace this default one with an icon that represents your app. Feel free to use any of those numerous online `favicon` generators to create your `favicon`. Remember that this `favicon` helps users to quickly identify your app within the multiple tabs of an open browser.
`app/index.html`	This will be the home page for your app. You can open it in a text editor to see what it contains. As you would have noticed, other than that one line of code with the `ng-views` directive, the rest of the file is mostly browser checks and inclusion of the various JavaScript files. Note that there is no actual AngularJS code other than `ng-views` and that's how it needs to be kept too.
`robots.txt`	This is the file where you set rules for the search engine robots or crawlers, telling them what pages they can index and which sections of the app should not be indexed.
`scripts/app.js`	This is the route's file where you'll define the template view and the controller that should load for a given URL. Controllers and views are loosely coupled in AngularJS; this means you can have a single controller talk to different views, or swap the templates for a controller by simply editing the routes in this `app.js` file.

`scripts/controllers/`
`main.js`
`scripts/controllers/`
`about.js`
	This is where you'll be writing the controllers for this app. As a part of the scaffolding, Yeoman would have already created a default `MainCtrl` and `AboutCtrl` controllers with a model created in each. Feel free to modify it and/or write the rest of your controllers in the same file.

`styles/main.css`	All your CSS code would go into this file. The `styles` folder would also contain the `bootstrap.css` file. This contains all the Bootstrap classes. Make sure you don't modify any of the code here or add any additional CSS in the bootstrap file.

Filename	Description
views/about.html views/main.html	The views folder would contain all the template views or partials as they are also called to load within the ng-views tag of the index.html file. The routes defined in the scripts/apps.js file would control what view will be displayed for the given URL.
Bower_components:	This contains folders for the various vendor libraries such as AngularJS, Angular Animate, jQuery, and Bootstrap and it is used for dependency management of these libraries.
bower.json	The bower.json file keeps a track of the dependencies and dev dependencies of the various modules and plugins for this app.
Gruntfile.js	You know what the Grunt file is for right? Open it in a text editor and be overwhelmed by the 300 plus lines of code in the file. You'll see a bunch of predefined tasks and you'll also notice that besides the default bundled task, you also have tasks called test and build. These can be used to preview your app and finally build it ready for deployment.
test/karma.conf.js	The karma.conf.js file is the configuration file for running Karma unit tests. Opening this file will show the testing framework we are using, list files that we want to include within the scope of these unit tests, what port to use, the browser to use, and so on.
node_modules	As self-explanatory as it can be, this folder contains the various Node.js modules that were defined in the package.json file. Note that these modules do not get installed when you run the yo-angular command. These would download and install only after you run the npm-install command after the creation of the package.json file.
package.json	This file lists out all the Node.js modules that need to be installed. You may edit this file with caution to add more or remove dependencies that you think are not needed for your app.
test/spec/ controllers/main.js	This is the file where you'd write the unit tests for your controllers. The main.js file would already have a simple unit test in it.
	The default configuration of Yeoman uses Jasmine; you can change the configurations to use Mocha or Qunit frameworks.

Let's install our Node.js modules by running the following command in the terminal:

```
npm install
```

Running your app

Earlier in this chapter, we saw how to set up a server using Node.js and ExpressJS. Yeoman comes with its own server and running it is as simple as running the following command in your terminal:

```
grunt serve
```

 The grunt server command is deprecated although it might still work for some.

This will open up a new browser window and will show you the default welcome screen, as shown in the following screenshot:

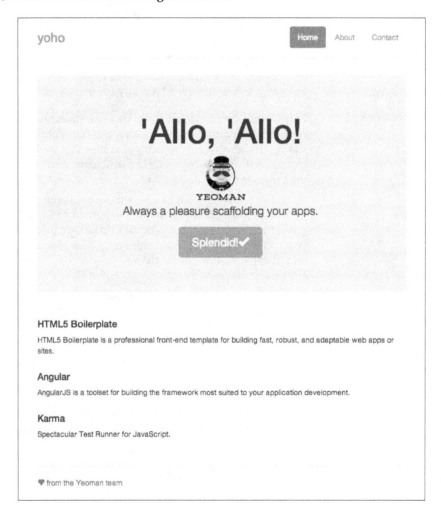

If you recollect looking at the `main.js` file (under `scripts/controllers`) and the `main.html` file (under `views`), you'll notice the page that is being rendered. Let's play around a bit.

Open the `scripts/controllers/main.js` file and you'll find a controller called `MainCtrl` and a model called `awesomeThings`. Let's add some more items to this array as follows:

```
'use strict';

angular.module('yohoApp')
  .controller('MainCtrl', function ($scope) {
    $scope.awesomeThings = [
      'HTML5 Boilerplate',
      'AngularJS',
      'Karma',
      'E2E',
      'Protractor'

    ];
  });
```

Let's display our `awesomeThings` array in the view. Please add the following code to the `main.html` file as follows:

```
<ul class="row">
    <li ng-repeat="things in awesomeThings">{{things}}</li>
</ul>
```

Save the file and switch to the browser. VOILA! The page updated on its own, you didn't have to reload the page in the browser.

The browser updates the moment you save your file, no more hitting the refresh button. Isn't that a big relief and a productivity boost!

This works thanks to a nifty module called `LiveReload`. You'll find this being installed as a part of `devDependencies` in the `package.json` file. You'll also notice Grunt tasks for it created in your `gruntfile.js` file.

So now you can have the server running and place your browser window and your text editor arranged side-by-side, and watch your app update as you write your code and save the file.

Unit testing with Karma

Writing automated unit tests for your AngularJS app is one of the best practices, the AngularJS team has been strongly advocating this right from the start. Every sample code on the www.Angularjs.org site has automated test cases along with it.

Keeping in line with the same philosophy, Yeoman too bakes in some sample unit tests using Karma. While Yeoman would automatically install Karma and its dependencies, let us, nevertheless, make sure the following modules are present in the node_modules folder:

- karma

- karma-chrome-launcher

- karma-jasmine

In case you don't find them in your node_modules folder, install them using the npm install command. Next, make sure your karma.conf.js file looks like the following:

```
module.exports = function(config) {
  config.set({
    basePath: '',
    frameworks: ['jasmine'],
    files: [
  'bower_components/angular/angular.js',
  'bower_components/angular-mocks/angular-mocks.js',
  'bower_components/angular-animate/angular-animate.js',
  'bower_components/angular-resource/angular-resource.js',
  'bower_components/angular-cookies/angular-cookies.js',
  'bower_components/angular-route/angular-route.js',
  'bower_components/angular-sanitize/angular-sanitize.js',
  'bower_components/angular-touch/angular-touch.js',
  'app/app.js',
  'app/scripts/*.js',
  'app/scripts/**/*.js',
  'test/spec/**/*.js'
    ],
    exclude: [

    ],
    preprocessors: {

    },
    reporters: ['progress'],
    port: 9876,
```

```
        colors: true,
        logLevel: config.LOG_INFO,
        autoWatch: true,
        browsers: ['Chrome'],
        singleRun: false
    });
};
```

To run your unit tests, simply run the following command in the terminal:

grunt test

This will fire up a new Chrome browser window and in the terminal start running through your tests. Refer to the following screenshot:

```
Running "karma:unit" (karma) task
INFO [karma]: Karma v0.12.16 server started at http://localhost:9876/
INFO [launcher]: Starting browser Chrome
WARN [watcher]: Pattern "/Users/vinci/book/ReWrites/Chapter 2/56170S_02_code/yoho/app/app.js" does no
t match any file.
INFO [Chrome 35.0.1916 (Mac OS X 10.9.2)]: Connected on socket 9BDdmeUz1pnbpvX94mYV with id 2567049
Chrome 35.0.1916 (Mac OS X 10.9.2) Controller: MainCtrl should attach a list of awesomeThings to the
scope FAILED
        Expected 5 to be 3.
        Error: Expected 5 to be 3.
            at null.<anonymous> (/Users/vinci/book/ReWrites/Chapter 2/56170S_02_code/yoho/test/spec/c
ontrollers/main.js:20:40)
Chrome 35.0.1916 (Mac OS X 10.9.2): Executed 2 of 2 (1 FAILED) (0.052 secs / 0.047 secs)
Warning: Task "karma:unit" failed. Use --force to continue.

Aborted due to warnings.


Execution Time (2014-06-14 19:37:20 UTC)
concurrent:test  3.4s  ████████████████████ 36%
karma:unit       5.9s  ███████████████████████████████████ 63%
Total 9.4s
```

Oh! We got an error in `MainCtrl`. It would say something like **Expected 5 to be 3** and point you to an error in the file located at `test/spec/controllers/main.js`.

Let's open up this file and see what's going on in there. The test case that's failing is as follows:

```
it('should attach a list of awesomeThings to the scope', function() {
    expect(scope.awesomeThings.length).toBe(3);
});
```

If you recollect, earlier we had modified our `awesomeThings` controller and added some additional elements to the array, the preceding test case is expecting the length of that array to be 3. Let's now modify that statement to the following code:

```
expect(scope.awesomeThings.length).toBeGreaterThan(3);
```

Let's save this file and rerun the following command:

```
grunt test
```

The test cases should run fine with a message saying **Executed 2 of 2 SUCCESS.......
Done**, without errors. We will be writing more unit tests with Karma in the
forthcoming chapters.

Using Protractor for End-to-End tests

As we saw earlier with Karma, we can write unit tests that will make sure that our
code in the controllers is working well; however, it would fall short if you wanted to
run automated **User Acceptance Tests** (**UAT**) or run tests that simulate user-driven
interactions with the browser. For running such tests, we'll need to use another new
tool called **Protractor**.

Protractor replaces the earlier AngularJS scenarios as the default End-to-End testing
framework for testing AngularJS apps.

Protractor runs on `WebDriver.js`, which in turn makes use of the **Selenium Server**.
Selenium is one of the most popular browser-automation tools. In this section, we
will see how to set up a standalone instance of Selenium Server, install Protractor,
and run a default set of End-to-End tests with it.

Let's first install Protractor by running the following command in the terminal:

```
sudo npm install -g protractor
```

This will install Protractor globally.

Installing Selenium Server

Protractor comes with a handy script called `webdriver-manager` that can be used
to download and run the Selenium Server.

In the terminal, type in the following command to download Selenium Server:

```
webdriver-manager update
```

To start the server, type in the following command:

```
webdriver-manager start
```

This should start your Selenium Server. Now open your browser and type in the
`http://localhost:4444/wd/hub/static/resource/hub.html` address in the
address bar. This will show you the current status of the Selenium Server.

The `protractor` folder within the `node_modules` comes with a couple of default tests that can help you jump start, writing your End-to-End tests. These tests are located in the `usr/local/lib/node_modules/protractor/example` folder.

Depending on what you are comfortable with, you can choose between Jasmine and Mocha for writing your test cases. From the `example` folder under `protractor`, copy the `conf.js` and the `example_spec.js` files and paste them into a new `test/protractor-tests` folder.

Understanding the example_spec.js file

The `example_spec.js` file is the specs file where the test cases are written. Let's open this file in an editor and try and make sense of what it is going to do.

We first describe our test suite as follows:

```
describe('angularjs homepage', function() { })
```

Next, let's look at the test case. The first test case looks something like the following:

```
it('should greet the named user', function() {
    browser.get('http://www.angularjs.org');

    element(by.model('yourName')).sendKeys('Julie');

    var greeting = element(by.binding('yourName'));

    expect(greeting.getText()).toEqual('Hello Julie!');
});
```

The first line describes the test case. In the next line, we navigate to the defined URL; in this case we load the `www.angularjs.org` home page.

Once the home page is loaded, in the next step the code is trying to locate an input field bound to a model called `yourName` and type in the text `Julie`. It then looks for the expression called `Hello{{yourName}}` and verifies that the text reads `Hello Julie`.

Let's look at the second test suite, which has two test cases as follows:

```
describe('todoList', function() {
    var todoList;
```

We define the suite name and initialize `todoList`. Now since both the test cases need to go to the same URL and will be based on `todoList`, we use `beforeEach` to set the URL and load the content into our `todoList` array as follows:

```
beforeEach(function() {
    browser.get('http://www.angularjs.org');

    todoList = element.all(by.repeater('todo in todos'));
});
```

The first test case checks to see if we have two items in `todoList` and that the second item is called `build an angular app`. Refer to the following code:

```
it('should list todos', function() {
    expect(todoList.count()).toEqual(2);
    expect(todoList.get(1).getText()).toEqual('build an angular
app');
});
```

The second test case will simulate adding an item to `todolist` by locating the `todoText` model, and adding in and verifying the text being added as follows:

```
it('should add a todo', function() {
    var addTodo = element(by.model('todoText'));
    var addButton = element(by.css('[value="add"]'));

    addTodo.sendKeys('write a protractor test');
    addButton.click();

    expect(todoList.count()).toEqual(3);
    expect(todoList.get(2).getText()).toEqual('write a protractor
test');
});

})
```

Understanding the conf.js file

The `conf.js` file is the configuration file. Open it in an editor and you'll see the configuration settings such as the default address for the Selenium Server, the base URL, the browser to be used for testing, and the location of your test cases. Now, since we have the `example_spec.js` file in the same path as our `conf.js` file, let's correct the path of the specs to read as follows:

```
specs: [example_spec.js'],
```

To run our test suite, open the terminal and navigate to the yoho folder and type in the following command:

```
protractor test/protractor-tests/conf.js
```

This will launch a browser instance and see the steps being performed by the script. The browser will automatically close once the script is executed and the terminal window should display the following message:

Finished in xxx.xxxx seconds

2 tests, 2 assertions, 0 failures

 Sometimes you might start getting errors like **Error: ECONNREFUSED connect ECONNREFUSED**. In such a case restart your Selenium Standalone Server and web server.

Writing your own Protractor test cases

Now that we know how test cases are written in Protractor and how to run them, let's quickly write a couple of our own test cases against the default scaffold application that Yeoman created for us.

Let's create a new file called mytests.js in the test folder under yoho/protractor-tests. Now we can start writing out our test cases as follows:

```
describe('our homepage', function() { })
```

The first test case we will write is the one where we'll check to see if the page heading within the h1 tags says 'Allo Allo!'. The test case for that would look something like the following:

```
it('should say Allo', function() {
    browser.get('http://localhost:9000/#/');
    var heading = element(by.tagName('h1'))
    expect(heading.getText()).toEqual("'Allo, 'Allo!")
});
```

The browser.get function defines the URL of the page you'd want Protractor to navigate to. We use the by.tagName selector to locate the h1 tag and get the text within it and verify that it matches "'Allo, 'Allo!".

Let's write our second test case. Here, we want to ensure that the width of our page is within the recommended limits and isn't going beyond the screen size of most common users. Refer to the following code:

```
it('should not be greater than 940px', function() {
    browser.get('http://localhost:9000/#/')
    element(by.className('container')).getSize().then(function(size) {
        expect(size.width).toBeLessThan(950)
    })
})
```

Here, we are using the by.className selector to identify the container div and using the getSize property we check to make sure that the width is not greater than 950px.

Notice that the .then() function is a part of a promise, which ensures that the code waits for the result to be returned. We'll see promises in detail in *Chapter 4, Using REST Web Services in Your AngularJS App*. For now, save the file.

Now that we have our test case's specs file ready, we need to call it within the protractor configuration file. Let's open the conf.js file and change the filename in the specs array to point to our mytest.js file as follows:

```
specs: ['mytests.js'],
```

We are now set to test our scripts. First, let's start our server by running the following command:

cd yoho

grunt serve

This should start our server. Now, let's run our protractor test script by running the following command from within the yoho folder:

protractor test/protractor-tests/conf.js

Make sure you have your Selenium Standalone Server running; if not, start it using the following command:

webdriver-manager start

If all goes well, you could see the Chrome browser being launched, and see the script navigate to the localhost:9000/#/ URL and the browser window closing down after some time.

Switch to your terminal to see the status saying the following in green that means our test cases worked:

Finished in x.xxx seconds

2 tests, 2 assertions, 0 failures

 In case you'd like to run your test cases without having to launch the browser window each time or if you'd want to run it headless on a server, then have a look at PhantomJS (`http://phantomjs.org/`), which is an excellent headless browser that runs on the WebKit engine.

Summary

This completes our chapter on setting up your rig. We worked through quite a few tools, namely Node.js, Grunt, Yeoman, Karma, and Protractor. While I strongly recommend making use of all of them when you build your AngularJS projects, you may feel free to choose the ones that suit your project the best.

Another thing to note is that most of these tools such as Node.js, ExpressJS, and Grunt can be used for any non-AngularJS projects. So getting familiar with these tools is surely beneficial for all frontend developers.

In the next chapter, we are going to see how to quickly build a clickable prototype using Angular-UI.

3
Rapid Prototyping with AngularJS

In the previous chapter, we saw how to set up the various tools that will aid in building our AngularJS app. In this chapter, we will see how AngularJS lends itself as an excellent tool to create prototypes.

Rapid Prototyping is an excellent way of validating the goals of the web application you are planning to build. It gives useful and important feedback from users and stakeholders on various aspects of the application, such as user click flows, usability issues, and usefulness of the requirement specifications that were initially outlined.

In the past, prototypes were built using either wireframing tools, or developers would create a series of HTML pages linked with each other that would mimic the functioning of the web application. While the former never gave the right feel of how the app would look and behave, the latter would take a much longer time to build, especially if it was a large application.

Now, thanks to AngularJS, building such prototypes has become a lot easier, and one can build nearly functional prototype within a short time frame and with significantly less code.

In this chapter, we will do the following:

- Run through the various components of the application that we are going to prototype
- Understand Grid Layouts and see how Bootstrap works
- Add UI components such as **carousels**, **accordions**, and **modal windows** using Angular UI
- Learn the modular way to build pages using **partials**
- Create dummy data models to simulate dynamic data
- Use routes to link the controllers to the views

Understanding the application that we will Prototype

We will create a clickable prototype of a pseudo web app named Healthy Living. It will consist of four pages. They are as follows:

- **Homepage**: This will consist of a carousel, hero unit, and three main content blocks.

- **Articles**: This display a list of articles in an accordion view.

- **Gallery**: This is an image gallery page with pictures, a title, a short description, and a star rating.

- **Subscribers**: This page will display the list of subscribers in an interactive data grid with features to group by a column and Excel-style inline editing. The subscription page will also have a button that will allow us to add a new user via a modal window.

Introducing Grid Layouts and Bootstrap

Building HTML pages had always been a web designer's job, and programmers would run miles away if asked to build an HTML page.

Another problem with designing HTML pages is that every designer has their own secret recipe to create an HTML page, using their own structure to lay out the DOM elements and their favorite CSS class names. This causes quite an anguish when developers take over HTML to put in the dynamic code, or when two designers are working on the same project.

The Grid Layouts evolved as a means to help get everybody on the same page in terms of naming conventions and the DOM structure, and more importantly, to reduce the time taken to build HTML pages while ensuring a fair amount of browser compatibility at the same time.

While grid systems such as the 960 Grid System and Blueprint were among the early grid systems available, nowadays, Bootstrap, Foundation, and Semantic UI have become very popular tools to build frontend pages.

At the time of writing this book, the version of Bootstrap that is compatible with Angular UI is 3.1.x, and we will be using this to build our prototype.

Understanding the grid system

Of late, grid systems have been extensively used in web-development workflows. Grid systems aim to streamline the HTML markup process by providing a standard set of dimensions and display styles for the commonly used UI elements. The following screenshot shows a grid system:

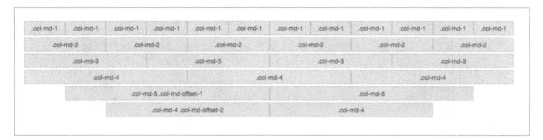

Bootstrap has a default 12-column grid system that is available as a responsive, fluid, and fixed layout. It comes with a complete set of predefined classes that meets nearly all your UI styling needs.

Some of the most commonly used classes are mentioned in the following table:

Class	Description
.col-md-*	This is for column widths that are applied to a content block for medium screen devices such as desktops with resolutions greater than or equal to 992 px wide.
.col-xs-*	This is for small devices with a width of 768 px or less.
.col-sm-*	This is for tablet devices with a size of 768 px or more.
.col-lg-*	This is for large devices with sizes greater than or equal to 1200 px.
.col-md-offset-*	The offset class is used to leave column spacing from the left.
.row .row-fluid	The .row class is used to separate the data row wise. The .row-fluid class is used in case of a fluid layout.
.container .container-fluid	The .container class will set the element width to 940 px and will center it horizontally with respect to the page. The .container-fluid class is used in case of a fluid layout.
.lead	This is used to make a paragraph stand out. It is most commonly used within a hero unit or to display the page summary under the page heading.

Class	Description
`.text-left` `.text-center` `.text-right`	These are used to align the text to the left, center and right respectively.
`<blockquote> </blockquote>` `<cite> </cite>`	The `<blockquote>` and `</blockquote>`tags are used to quote somebody, and the `<cite>` and `</cite>` tags are used to wrap the name of the source.
`.pull-left` `.pull-right`	These are used to float an element and push it either to the left or right of its bounding container.
`.btn primary` `.btn-success` `.btn-info` `.btn-warning` `.btn-danger` `.btn-inverse`	These are used to style the buttons or anchor elements; these classes apply different colors to the button ranging from blue to black.

At the most minimum, Bootstrap comes with a CSS and JavaScript file along with an image (`/img`) folder containing the **glyphicons**. The CSS file contains all the styles for the grid system and the predefined classes for the various UI components. JavaScript contains the libraries to build UI widgets such as accordions, tabs, modal windows, progress bars, date pickers, and so on.

Introducing Angular UI

Angular UI is a bunch of mini projects that helps you be more productive with your Angular app development. At the time of writing this book, Angular UI consisted of projects discussed in the following sections.

UI-Utils

UI-Utils is a utility package that allows you to add a wide variety of utilities into your application. The utilities are explained as follows:

- **IE Shiv**: This is used to allow support for custom tags in IE8 and below.
- **jQuery Passthrough**: The `uiJq` directive allows us to use jQuery plugins directly instead of having to create new directives to use them.
- **Event Binder**: This allows you to bind callbacks to events that are not natively supported in AngularJS.

- **Keypress**: This allows you to bind events to a keypress.

- **Mask**: This allows you to mask data based on certain conditions set.

- **Validate**: This allows you to create custom validators and expressions

- **Reset**: This allows you to display an icon or link; if you click on it, the model will become empty.

- **Scrollfix**: This adds a `ui-scrollfix` class to the element.

- **Show / Hide / Toggle**: This allows you to use a single directive of `ui-toggle` instead of using `ng-show` and `ng-hide`.

- **Route Matching**: This is a nifty little directive that can be used to match the route of the current page.

- **Highlight**: This is used to highlight a string of characters within a scope model.

- **Inflector**: This will help you convert a string into alternative formats such as replace spaces with underscores or convert the string into a `camelCase` syntax.

- **Unique**: This can be used to remove all duplicate items from within an array.

- **Format**: This filter can be used to do any kind of string replacement.

UI-Modules

The UI-Modules project allows you to easily add Calendar Controls, Google Maps, and a bunch of editors such as **TinyMCE** and **CodeMirror Ace**.

UI-Bootstrap

UI-Bootstrap is the native implementation of Twitter Bootstrap within Angular. As we'll see further in this chapter, adding UI controls, such as carousels, accordions, and tabs, is a breeze using UI-Bootstrap. It is worth noting that UI-Bootstrap uses the original CSS and glyphicons of Bootstrap as they are. It's only the JavaScript file that has been rewritten to use native Angular directives.

NG-Grid

NG-Grid allows you to add data grids in your Angular app. NG-Grid comes with quite a few customization options that allow you to place grids with sortable columns to features such as Excel-style editing, in place.

UI-Router

UI-Router is a new way of routing that allows you to create **Nested Routing**.

IDE Plugins

IDE Plugins are a bunch of plugins or extensions that provide AngularJS support in various text editors.

As we move ahead in the chapter, we will make extensive use of the UI-Bootstrap and NG-Grid projects.

Prototyping the Healthy Living website

For this exercise, we are going to create a four-page clickable prototype of a pseudo website called Healthy Living. The home page will consist of a fully functional carousel, hero unit, and three content sections with call to actions. The following screenshot is that of the home page:

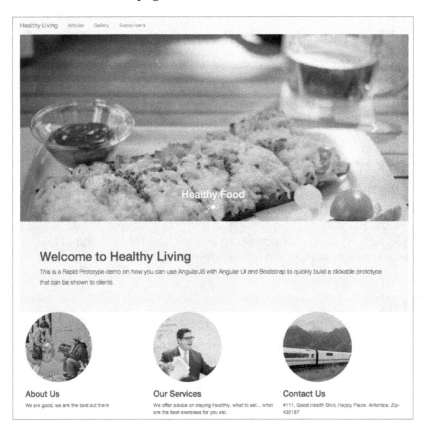

Let's get started with the creation of our application. We'll start by performing the following steps:

1. Create a folder named `hl`, short for "Healthy Living".

2. Assuming that you have already installed Yeoman, open up the terminal. Let's create the scaffolding for our app using the following lines of code:

```
mkdir hl

cd hl

yo angular
```

> **Generator-Angular** must be installed before you can run your Angular app. In case you haven't installed it during *Chapter 2, Setting Up Your Rig*, please install it using the following command:
>
> ```
> sudo npm install -g generator-angular
> ```

3. In the prompt, press Y for the question, **Would you like to include Twitter Bootstrap?**.

4. For the question, **Would you like to use Sass (with Compass)?**, press N.

5. For the third question, press *Enter* to accept the default settings.

> Using a CSS preprocessor such as SASS or LESS is always a good practice as it allows you to use variables and mixins in CSS, ensuring that your CSS remains modular and follows **DRY (Don't Repeat Yourself)** principals. However, covering them is beyond the scope of this book.

You should be seeing npm pulling a bunch of files and creating the scaffold of your app. Wait patiently until it is all done and you are returned back to the command prompt.

You should now be able to see the structure of your application with the default home page.

As we are going to be using UI-Bootstrap, let's install it using Bower.

6. Fire the following command in the terminal:

```
bower install angular-bootstrap
```

This will create the `angular-bootstrap` folder within the `app/bower_components` folder.

To be able to use Angular Bootstrap in our application, we need to include the JS file.

7. Let's open up the `app/index.html` file and add the following highlighted line.

```
<script src="bower_components/jquery/dist/jquery.js"></script>
<script src="bower_components/angular/angular.js"></script>
<script src="bower_components/angular-bootstrap/ui-bootstrap-tpls.
js"></script>
```

If you look into the `bower_components/angular-bootstrap` folder, you'll notice there are the following two types of files along with their minified versions:

- **ui-bootstrap.js**: This contains all the directives, but it doesn't contain any templates. It makes sense to use this file if you do not want to use the default templates but want to customize your templates from scratch.

- **ui-bootstrap-tpls.js**: This contains all the directives along with the default twitter bootstrap template code. If you are not looking to make any customization, then its best to include this file in your project.

Adding the ui.bootstrap dependency

The next step is to add the Angular Bootstrap dependency to the Angular app.

We do this by modifying the following line in the `app/scripts/app.js` file:

```
angular.module('hlApp', ['ui.bootstrap'])
```

Now, `angular-bootstrap` will be available for use across our application.

Creating the navigation bar

To create the navigation bar, let's open up the `app/index.html` file and add the `<nav>` part of the code, which is shown as follows:

```
<nav class="navbar navbar-default navbar-fixed-top">
    <div class="container">
        <a class="navbar-brand" href="/">Healthy Living</a>

        <ul class="nav navbar-nav">
            <li> <a href="/#/articles">Articles</a>
            </li>
            <li> <a href="/#/gallery">Gallery</a>
            </li>
            <li> <a href="/#/subscribers">Subscribers</a>
```

```
        </li>

      </ul>
    </div>
  </nav>
  <!-- Add your site or application content here -->
    <div class="container" ng-view=""></div>
```

As you can see from the preceding code, we defined the header tag and applied the CSS classes, navbar and navbar-fixed-top, to it. These are predefined bootstrap CSS classes that are used to style the navigation bar.

The navbar class is a default container that sets the overflow to visible for all elements within the navbar DOM.

The navbar-fixed-top class will make the navigation bar stick to the top of the page, and it will stay fixed even as the page scrolls. You can also use navbar-fixed-bottom to make your navigation bar stick to the bottom of the page.

Now, we'll add the <div> tag with a class named container. The container class will set the width of this element to 940 px and also center the element horizontally on the page.

We will add our Healthy Living website within an anchor tag and give it a class named navbar-brand, as this is what our brand name is supposed to be.

Navigation links for the **Articles**, **Gallery**, and **Subscribers** pages will be added as hyperlinks within an unordered list, which is styled using the nav class. Note the '/#/' in the href values.

Save the file and start the server using the following command:

grunt serve

This will run the serve task defined within our Gruntfile.js file. You should now be able to see the navigation bar at the top of the page.

Adding the carousel

Now, let's see how to add a carousel using angular-bootstrap. I'm sure most of you would have added carousels in your project. Most probably, these would have been one of those numerous jQuery plugins, and I'm sure that some of you must have struggled to make it work the first time.

Angular Bootstrap has its own custom directive for carousel and it's extremely easy to add a carousel to your home page using it.

As the home page is rendered using the `MainCtrl` controller and the `views/main.html` partial, we will be adding our carousel code to these files.

In the past, one of the biggest drawbacks of creating HTMLized click flows has been the intermingling of design and data. Most designers would create regular HTML pages with static markups linked with each other. The problem with this is, besides a lot of repetitive code, when these click flows are taken up to create the actual app, there is a fair amount of rework that would need to be done.

Now, with Angular, it becomes extremely easy to separate your presentation layer from the actual data. Besides making this very efficient to write, it also becomes very easy to take this for actual development, as one now needs to only replace the static data models with the dynamic data; the presentation layers don't need to be changed at all.

With the idea of keeping the data separate from the markup, let's first create our data models in the `app/scripts/controllers/main.js` file.

We will delete the current `awesomeThings` model and start replacing it with the following code:

```
var baseURL='http://lorempixel.com/960/450/';
$scope.setInterval=5000;
```

Now, when you create any kind of website or mockup, there is always a need to use placeholder images or stock images. There is an excellent site called `www.lorempixel.com` that provides images of the desired dimensions and for a certain category.

It is extremely easy to use **lorempixel** where you want to display placeholder images. For example, use `http://lorempixel.com/960/450/sports`, where `960` and `450` are the width and height, respectively, of the desired image, and the category is sports. Visit `www.lorempixel.com` to see the list of category keywords they support.

As we are going to be using images from here, we'll define a variable named `baseURL` with the URL string passing the `width` and `height` parameters that we want for the image.

Next, we create another variable called `setInterval` with a value of `5000`. This will be used to set the autoslider of the carousel to 5 seconds.

Now, we'll create our `slides` model using the following lines of code:

```
$scope.slides = [
    {
        title:'7 Ways to stay Fit',
        image:baseURL+'sports/',
```

```
        text:'Play a sport for 30 minutes a day!'
    },
    {

        title:'Healthly Food',
        image:baseURL+'food/',
        text:'Food that you should be eating!'
    },
    {

        title:'Relaxing Holidays',
        image:baseURL+'nature/',
        text:'10 Locations for Nature Lovers!'
    }


    ];
```

This is essentially a JavaScript object with three parameters, namely `title`, `image`, and `text`. Note that for the `image` property, we prefix the term `baseURL` to the category name for each of the slides. This completes our work on the model.

Now, let's first open the `views/main.html` file and add the following markup above the `jumbotron` element:

```
<carousel interval="setInterval">
   <slide ng-repeat="slide in slides" active="slide.active">
   </slide>
</carousel>
```

As you can see, this is a custom directive called `<carousel>` that has been natively written in `angular-bootstrap`.

The `interval` attribute is used to set a delay between each slide change as follows:

```
interval=setInterval
```

We then loop though the slides using `ng-repeat`.

Now, we'll put in the elements that will display the image, title, and text. Within the `<slides>` tag, add the following code:

```
<img class="carousel-image" ng-src="{{slide.image}}"/>
<div class="carousel-caption">
      <h2>{{slide.title}}</h2>
      <p>{{slide.text}}</p>
</div>
```

Save the files and watch the browser refresh automatically (*this happens if you have the server still running*).

You should now be able to see the slider working.

You'll notice that the navigation bar is overlapping the carousel. This is because of the `position:absolute` property that gets applied when we add the `navbar-top-fixed` class.

You'll also notice that on wide-screen monitors, the carousel image doesn't cover the entire width. This happens because by default, Bootstrap works in the responsive mode and will change the container width to 1170 px while our carousel image is 960 px.

To fix these problems, we'll add the following CSS classes. In the `app/styles/ main.css` file, delete the present code and add the following lines of code:

```
body{
   padding-top: 50px;
}

.carousel-image{
   width: 100%;
}
```

Tweaking the hero unit

OK. Now, let's clean up our hero unit and put in some decent text. Let's open the `app/views/main.html` file and change the content within the hero unit element as follows:

```
<div class="hero-unit">
  <h1>Welcome to Healthy Living</h1>
  <p>This is a Rapid Prototype demo on how you can use AngularJS
  with Angular UI and Bootstrap to quickly build a clickable
  prototype that can be shown to clients</p>
</div>
```

You'll notice that the hero unit is quite narrow and feels claustrophobic; we can make it look nicer by adding the following class in the `styles/main.css` file.

```
.hero-unit {
    font-size: 18px;
    font-weight: 200;
    line-height: 30px;
    background-color: #eee;
```

```
border-radius: 6px;
padding: 60px;
}
```

Adding the three content blocks

Things are taking shape! Let's now add the three blocks under the hero unit. We will use the same approach of keeping the data within the model and the markup in the partial.

Open up the `app/scripts/controllers/main.js`, and let's create another model named `content`, as we want to use images from **lorempixel** there too. We will follow the same structure for the `content` model as we did for the `slides` model.

Add the following code for the `content` model just after the `slides` model:

```
// Model for the 3 content blocks
var baseURL='http://lorempixel.com/200/200/'
$scope.content=[
{
    img:baseURL+'people',
    title:'About Us',
    summary:'We are good, we are the best out there'
},
{
    img:baseURL+'business',
    title:'Our Services',
    summary:'We offer advice on staying Healthly, what to eat...
    what are the best exercises for you etc.'
},
{

    img:baseURL+'transport',
    title:'Contact Us',
    summary:'#111, Good Health Blvd, Happy Place, Antartica,
Zip-432167'
}
]
```

Here, we are using 200 x 200 px size images from `lorempixel.com`.

The structure of the model object is very similar to that of `slides`, so understanding this should be easy.

Now, let's add the markup in our `app/views/main.html` partial.

After the hero unit markup, let's create the `row` container that will contain the following `<div>` tags for the three blocks:

```
<div class="row-fluid">

</div>
```

To create the three blocks, we'll need three containers, and each of them would be four columns wide.

 As the default Bootstrap is 12 columns wide, the width for each of the three columns is simply *12 / 3 = 4*.

Within the `row-fluid` class, let's create the markup for one of the blocks which we will repeat using `ng-repeat`. The code is as follows:

```
<div class="col-md-4" ng-repeat="block in content">
        <img ng-src="{{block.img}}">
        <h3>{{block.title}}</h3>
        <p>{{block.summary}} </p>
</div>
```

Save the file and load the page on your browser to see the changes take effect.

Things look OK, but those square images within the blocks don't look that great; maybe we should put them within circles.

With Bootstrap, it's just a question of adding the `img-circle` class to the `<img>` tag as follows:

```
<img class="img-circle" ng-src="{{block.img}}">
```

Save the file and ensure that the images within the three blocks are now in a circle. In case you want the images with a rounded corner or with a polaroid effect, then simply replace the `img-circle` class with `img-rounded` or `img-polaroid`.

This completes the home page.

Creating a new view

Ideally, I'd call it a page, but as what we are building is a single-page app, we don't technically have different pages. What we do have are views, wherein a view is nothing but a unique URL or route that is linked to a controller and its corresponding partial.

To create a new articles view/page using Yeoman, we simply need to run the following subgenerator command in the terminal:

```
yo angular:route articles
```

You'll now notice that Yeoman has automatically performed the following set of actions:

- Created a new controller named `articles.js` within `app/scripts/controllers`
- Created a new partial named `articles.html` within `app/views/`
- Created the files for unit tests within `test/spec/controllers/articles.js`
- Modified the `app/scripts/app.js` file and added it in the routes for the articles view

Now, isn't that a lot of manual work you have been saved from!

To know more about the list of generators and subgenerators available on your system, use the following command line:

```
yo -help
```

Yeoman also allows you to create your own generators. The following link gives out more information on how to create or extend a generator:

```
http://yeoman.io/authoring/
```

Understanding routes

Routes play a very important role in your AngularJS app. The routes essentially tell AngularJS what controller and view to use for the given browser URL.

In our application, the routes are stored in the `app/scripts/app.js` file.

Routes make use of $routeProvider, and each route has two parameters: the first parameter is the path and the second is an object parameter. The following lines of code are entered under $routeProvider:

```
$routeProvider
  .when('/', {
    templateUrl: 'views/main.html',
    controller: 'MainCtrl'
  })
```

The when part defines the URL in the browser address bar. The templateURL part points to the partial that would be called within the ng-view directive. The controller part defines the controller function that will bind this view.

In AngularJS, the views and controllers are loosely coupled. What this means is that controllers and views are independent of each other, and it is in the routes file that a controller is linked to the view. So, essentially, you could have two different views bound to a single controller. This improves code reusability.

After the completion of this chapter, your routes would look something like the following.

```
'use strict';

angular.module('hlApp', ['ui.bootstrap','ngGrid'])
    .config(function ($routeProvider) {
        $routeProvider
            .when('/', {
                templateUrl: 'views/main.html',
                controller: 'MainCtrl'
            })
            .when('/articles', {
                templateUrl: 'views/articles.html',
                controller: 'ArticlesCtrl'
            })
            .when('/gallery', {
                templateUrl: 'views/gallery.html',
                controller: 'GalleryCtrl'
            })
            .when('/subscribers', {
                templateUrl: 'views/subscribers.html',
                controller: 'SubscribersCtrl'
            })
            .otherwise({
                redirectTo: '/'
            });
    });
```

The 'use strict' command that you see at the start of most of our files is a new feature of ECMAScript 5, which makes the file or function operate in a strict context. You can read more about it at https://developer.mozilla.org/en-US/docs/Web/JavaScript/Reference/Functions_and_function_scope/Strict_mode.

Building the articles view

Let's create the articles view by first creating our data model within the `app/scripts/controllers/articles.js` file.

Let's delete the default `awesomeThings` array and replace it with the following lines of code:

```
$scope.posts = [
{
title:"Almonds are good for Health",
content:"Almonds contain high amounts of HDL which helps reduce
cholestrol.Lorem ipsum dolor sit amet, consectetur adipiscing elit.
Vivamus rhoncus quam leo, id tristique sapien viverra eu. Maecenas
ipsum lectus, suscipit auctor tristique in, venenatis ut nisl. Quisque
eget bibendum libero. Nam nec mi augue."
},
{
title:"Sugar is bad for health",
content:"Sugar besides being bad for diabetes, it also causes
overweight and obesity problems. Lorem ipsum dolor sit amet,
consectetur adipiscing elit. Vivamus rhoncus quam leo, id tristique
sapien viverra eu. Maecenas ipsum lectus, suscipit auctor tristique
in."
},
{
title:"Cut down your carbs!!!",
content:"Sugar besides being bad for diabetes, it also causes
overweight and obesity problems.Lorem ipsum dolor sit amet,
consectetur adipiscing elit. Vivamus rhoncus quam leo, id tristique
sapien viverra eu. Maecenas ipsum lectus, suscipit auctor tristique
in, venenatis ut nisl. Quisque eget bibendum libero. Nam nec mi
augue."
        }

        ];
```

By now, I'm sure you are well versed of the structure of the preceding data model.

With regard to generating the dummy lorem lipsum text, `www.lipsum.com` is one of the best places to generate your summary text. Nowadays, many IDEs too have snippets, plugins, or macros to generate the lorem lipsum code.

Lorem lipsum was invented sometime in the 1500s when an unknown printer took a galley of type and scrambled it to make a type specimen book. Since then, it has been used extensively in the type setting and printing industry and has also made it into the electronic age.

Accordions using Angular Bootstrap

Now that our model is ready, let's get to the partial. We will display the preceding model data within an accordion.

As per our routes setting, `ArticlesCtrl` is mapped to the `views/articles.html` file; hence, we'll write our markup in this file.

Open the `app/views/articles.html` file and write the following code:

```
<h1>Articles</h1>
<accordion>
    <accordion-group heading=" {{post.title}}" ng-repeat="post in
    posts">
            {{post.content}}
    </accordion-group>
</accordion>
```

The first line sets the page title within the Heading tag.

Next, we call our directive to display the accordion. The `<accordion>` tag can contain multiple `<accordion-group>` sections, each with a heading attribute and a body area.

Using `ng-repeat`, we simply loop through the rows of data in our model and place them within the heading and content area.

Save the file and navigate the browser to see your `articles` page in action. It should look something like the following screenshot:

Building the image gallery

The next step is to build our image gallery, so let's create the controller, partial, and routes for it using the Yeoman command as follows:

```
yo angular:route gallery
```

We will start with the creation of our model in the `app/scripts/controllers/gallery.js` file.

This time, rather than creating static object models in the controller, we'll define a set of arrays and create our model dynamically. This would be a much more efficient way of building the models, especially if you have a large amount of data.

Let's start by defining the various variables and arrays that we will need within the `GalleryCtrl` controller function as follows:

```
var pictures =$scope.pictures=[];

var baseURL="http://lorempixel.com/300/180/";

var titles=["Healthy Food","Healthy @ Work","City Life ",
            "Staying Fit","Looking Good","Nightlife !!"] ;

var keywords=["food", "business","city","sports","fashion",
            "nightlife"];

var dummyText="Lorem ipsum dolor sit amet, consectetur adipiscing

            elit. Sed sed erat turpis. Integer eget

            consectetur quam. Sed at quam ut dolor varius

            condimentum et sit amet odio. "
```

First, we declare an empty model named `pictures`.

The next variable we define is `baseURL`, which holds the base URL for the images that we will show in the image gallery. As you can notice, in this case, we are using images of width 300 and height 180.

Next, `titles` is the array containing the titles for all the images.

The `keywords` array holds the list of all the keywords that we will concatenate at the end of `baseURL` to get relevant images for the gallery.

Finally, the `dummyText` variable holds some lorem ipsum text that we will add as a description to each of the gallery images.

Now that we have all the variables and arrays defined, the next step is to create the function that will push them into the `pictures` model.

The function is defined as follows:

```
$scope.addPics=function(i){
    pictures.push({
        url:baseURL+keywords[i],
        title:titles[i],
        summary:dummyText
    })
}
```

The `addPics` function takes in an input parameter `i`, which does an array push by iterating through the arrays and updating the values for the `url`, `title`, and `summary` properties.

The final step here is to call the `addPics` function in a loop, incrementing the value of `i`. This is done as follows:

```
for (var i=0;i<5;i++){
    $scope.addPics(i);
}
```

As, for this example, we need about six images, we run a for loop iterating from 0 to 5.

This completes our work on the controller. Now, let's look at the markup for the gallery partial.

Gallery view using Bootstrap Thumbnail

Angular Bootstrap doesn't have any special directive to create or display the thumbnails for the gallery view; hence, we will be using the regular Bootstrap classes to create our view.

Let's open the `views/gallery.html` file and write the following code:

```
<h1>Gallery</h1>
<div class="thumbnails">
    <div class="col-md-4" ng-repeat="pic in pictures">
```

```
        <img ng-src="{{pic.url}}">
        <h3>{{pic.title}}</h3>
        <p> {{pic.summary}}</p>
    </div>
</div>
```

Save the file and switch to your browser to see your gallery page in action. Ensure your images take the full width of the column by adding the following CSS lines:

```
.thumbnails img{
width:100%}
```

 In case the page doesn't show up, open up the console either in Firebug or Chrome developer tools to see if any JavaScript errors are throwing up. Try and fix these errors to get your page to work.

Adding the star rating

Let's make our gallery page a little more interesting by adding in the star rating feature. Thanks to Angular Bootstrap, adding this feature is as simple as adding one line of code in the partial. So, let's open up the app/views/gallery.html file and add the following highlighted line:

```
<h1>Gallery</h1>
<div class="thumbnails">
    <div class="col-md-4" ng-repeat="pic in pictures">
    <img src="{{pic.url}}">
    <rating ng-model="rate" max="max" readonly="isReadonly" ></rating>
        <h3>{{pic.title}}</h3>
        <p> {{pic.summary}}</p>
    </div>
</div>
```

In the app/scripts/controllers/gallery.js controller, we simply need to define the following values

```
$scope.rate = 0;
$scope.max = 10;
$scope.isReadonly = false;
```

Save the file and view the gallery page in the browser. It should now look like the following screenshot:

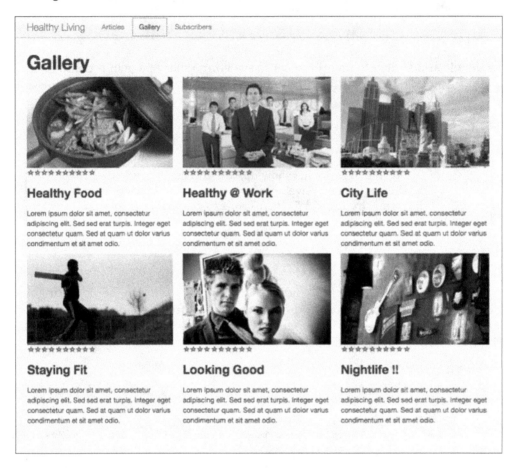

Building data grids using NG-Grid

Tables or data grids are something that we need to add in our applications quite often. At the beginning, creating tables is fairly simple; you simply create a `<table>` tag and populate the rows and columns. However, as you proceed, things get complicated; you will be asked to allow sorting on columns, or you will have to paginate through multiple rows and, at times, you will even be asked to allow inline editing like Excel.

Thanks to NG-Grid, creating such feature-rich data grids in AngularJS has become very easy.

Adding the NG-Grid component

NG-Grid is not a part of Angular Bootstrap and needs to be added separately. Let's use Bower to download the components for NG-Grid. In your terminal, navigate to your project folder, and type in the following command lines:

```
cd hl
bower install ng-grid
```

You should now be able to see the `ng-grid` folder and the files within the `bower_components` folder.

The next thing is to include the `ng-grid` JS and CSS files in our `index.html` file. Add the following highlighted line in your `app/index.html` file to include the `ng-grid` CSS file:

```
<link rel="stylesheet" href="styles/bootstrap.css">
<link rel="stylesheet" href="bower_components/ng-grid/ng-grid.css">
<link rel="stylesheet" href="styles/main.css">
```

> Make sure that the `main.css` file is the last file being called so that whatever style customization that you write in the `main.css` overrides the others.

Add the `ng-grid` JS file as highlighted in the following code snippet:

```
<script src="bower_components/jquery/dist/jquery.js"></script>
<script src="bower_components/angular/angular.js"></script>
<script src="bower_components/angular-bootstrap/ui-bootstrap-tpls.
js"></script>
<script src="bower_components/ng-grid/ng-grid-2.0.11.min.js"></script>
```

Next, we need to add the `ngGrid` dependency to `hlApp`. We'll do this by adding it in our `app/scripts/app.js` file as follows:

```
angular.module('hlApp', ['ui.bootstrap','ngGrid'])
```

Now that we have NG-Grid added to our projects, let's create the routes, controllers, and partials for the `subscribers` page.

Open up the terminal and run the following command:

`yo angular:route subscribers`

Once we are done with this, we are all set to start working on our `subscribers` view.

In most practical cases, we would call a web service that would return the list of subscribers. We can simulate a web service response by creating a static JSON file and putting in some dummy values.

Let's create a file in the app folder named `subscribers.json` and add in the following dummy JSON data:

```
[
{"no": "1","name":"Betty", "loyalty": 3,"joinDate":"3/5/10"},
{"no": "2","name":"John", "loyalty": 5,"joinDate":"3/5/05"},
{"no": "3","name":"Peter", "loyalty": 6,"joinDate":"3/5/10"},
{"no": "4","name":"Jaden", "loyalty": 7,"joinDate":"10/12/12"},
{"no": "5","name":"Shannon", "loyalty": 9,"joinDate":"22/01/08"}
]
```

Let's see how to load this data into our controller.

Add the following highlighted code within the `SubscribersCtrl` controller located in the `app/scripts/subscribers.js` file:

```
.controller('SubscribersCtrl', function ($scope,$http) {
$http.get('http://localhost:9000/subscribers.json').
success(function(data){
    $scope.subscribers =data
})
})
```

From the preceding code, you'll notice that we are injecting the `$http` service into our controller, and we use the `$http.get` method to make an HTTP request to the `subscribers.json` file.

The `$http` service will return a promise that contains two methods, namely `success` and `error`.

Within the `success` method, we populate our `subscribers` model with the returned data.

 We will be covering the `$http` service and the concept of `promise` in detail in *Chapter 4, Using REST Web Services in Your AngularJS App*.

Now that the model is ready, we need to initialize NG-Grid, so let's initialize `ng-grid` as follows:

```
$scope.gridOptions = {
    data: 'subscribers'
};
```

Our work on the controller is done. Let's open the `app/views/subscribers.html` partial and add the markup for the grid using the following lines of code.

```
<h1>Subscribers</h1>
<div class="gridStyles" ng-grid="gridOptions">
</div>
```

We'll also need to define the width and height of the grid. We'll do this by setting the width and height properties in the CSS.

Open up the `app/styles/main.css` file and add the `height` and `width` properties to the `.gridStyles` class.

```
.gridStyles{
    width:940px;
    height:300px;
}
```

 It is important to define at least the `height` property so that NG-Grid knows the area within which it should render the grid. If you miss out the `height` property, NG-Grid will by default take the height of the parent container, which sometimes will display just one row of data when you scroll.

Save the file and refresh the browser to see NG-Grid in action. Click on the column headings to see them sorted.

 Sometimes, you'll need to do a hard refresh to let NG-Grid know about any CSS changes that you would have made.

Right now, NG-Grid uses the model property names as the column headings. Many a times, this would not be ideal as one would want to define their own custom headers. This is possible by defining the `Column Definitions` property in `gridOptions`.

To add the `Column Definitions` property, open the `app/scripts/controllers/subscribers.js` file and add the following highlighted code:

```
$scope.gridOptions = {
    data: 'subscribers',
        columnDefs: [
        {field:'no', displayName:'No.'},
        {field:'name', displayName:'Name'},
```

```
                  {field:'loyalty', displayName:'Loyalty Score'},
                  {field:'joinDate', displayName:'Date of Joining'}]
       };
```

Save the file and navigate to the browser to see the new column heading take effect.

Now, the obvious question that arises is: how do we customize the alternating row colors? This can be done by simply overriding the default odd and even row classes by adding the following classes to the app/styles/main.css file:

```
.ngRow.even {
    background: AliceBlue;
}
.ngRow.odd {
    background: YellowGreen;
}
```

This should now give you a table grid with alternating rows of light-blue and green backgrounds.

Grouping data in NG-Grid

The NG-Grid is quite feature-rich, and besides the regular column sorting and alternating rows, it also allows for features such as the grouping of data by a column and Excel-style inline editing.

Let's see how data grouping in NG-Grid works. For this to look better and work more efficiently let's create a new attribute called Subscription Type in our models and use it for grouping.

Let's add a new property to our subscribers list in our subscribers.json file as highlighted in the following lines of code:

```
[
{"no":"1", "name":"Betty", "loyalty": 3,"joinDate":"3/5/10",
"userType":"Free"},
{"no":"2", "name":"John", "loyalty": 5,"joinDate":"3/5/05",
"userType":"Premium"},
{"no":"3", "name":"Peter", "loyalty": 6,"joinDate":"3/5/10",
"userType":"Free"},
{"no":"4", "name":"Jaden", "loyalty": 7,"joinDate":"10/12/12",
"userType":"Premium"},
{"no":"5", "name":"Shannon", "loyalty": 9,"joinDate":"22/01/08",
"userType":"Premium"}
]
```

We'll also add it to the column definitions in the gridOptions settings.

```
$scope.gridOptions = {
    data: 'subscribers',
        columnDefs: [
        {field:'no', displayName:'No.'},
        {field:'name', displayName:'Name'},
        {field:'userType', displayName:'Subscription Type'},
        {field:'loyalty', displayName:'Loyalty Score'},
        {field:'joinDate', displayName:'Date of Joining'}]

};
```

Save the file and verify that the **Subscription Type** column is now visible on the Subscriptions view.

Now, we'd like the user to drag a column into the group area and group the rows based on the selected column, something like the data-filters feature in the Excel Pivot tables.

Enabling this in NG-Grid is very simple; you simply need to add the following parameter to gridOptions in app/scripts/controllers/subscribers.js as highlighted in the following lines of code:

```
$scope.gridOptions = {
    data: 'subscribers',
    showGroupPanel: true,
    columnDefs: [
        {field:'no', displayName:'No.'},
        {field:'name', displayName:'Name'},
        {field:'userType', displayName:'Subscription Type'},
        {field:'loyalty', displayName:'Loyalty Score'},
        {field:'joinDate', displayName:'Date of Joining'}]

};
```

Save the file and refresh the Subscriptions view in your browser. You should now see a new area above the column headings. Drag the **Subscription Type** column heading and drop it in the area above it.

Note that the data in your grid has been grouped on the basis of the subscription type, and it also tells you the total number of users within each group. This is demonstrated in the following screenshot:

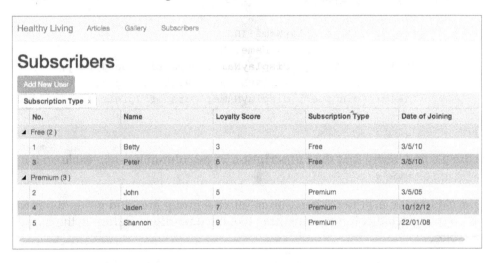

Excel-style editing in NG-Grid

I'm sure many of you come across this requirement where you need to allow for inline editing within a data grid. Trying to do this using the regular jQuery and Ajax can be quite an effort. Now, with NG-Grid, it's just about enabling these settings within `gridOptions`.

Open the `app/scripts/controllers/subscribers.js` file and add the following highlighted parameter to `gridOptions`:

```
$scope.gridOptions = {
    data: 'subscribers',
    showGroupPanel: true,
    jqueryUIDraggable: true,
    enableCellSelection: true,
    enableRowSelection: false,
    enableCellEdit: true,
    columnDefs: [
        {field:'no', displayName:'No.'},
        {field:'name', displayName:'Name'},
        {field:'userType', displayName:'Subscription Type'},
        {field:'loyalty', displayName:'Loyalty Score'},
        {field:'joinDate', displayName:'Date of Joining'}]

};
```

Save the file, and in the `Subscriptions` view in the browser, try double-clicking on any one of the cells, change the text, and press *Enter*. As simple as that! The following screenshot is the output obtained:

Creating a modal window to add subscribers

Now that we have a feature-rich data grid displaying our subscribers, let's create a modal window with a form to add users to our `subscribers` model.

Adding a modal window using Angular UI is a little more complicated than the rest of the components we have seen until now.

To start with, we will need a button that will launch the modal window when it is clicked on.

We will create this button in the `app/views/subscribers.html` file with the following highlighted lines of code:

```
<h1>Subscribers</h1>
<button class="btn btn-success" ng-click="showModal()"> Add New User</
button>
<div class="gridStyles" ng-grid="gridOptions">
</div>
```

The `.btn` class sets the button's basic styles such as rounded corners, font size, padding, and so on. The `.btn-success` class gives it the green color. In the `ng-click` directive, we are calling a function named `showModal`.

We will now create the partial for the modal view. Create a new file called add-user.html within the app/views folder, and let's put in the markup for the Add New User form as follows:

```
<div class="modal-header">
    <button type="button" class="close" ng-click="cancel()" data-
dismiss="modal" aria-hidden="true">&times;</button>
    <h1>Add a Subscriber</h1>
</div>
```

We define the heading for the modal window by applying the .modal-header class.

We also place our close button within the header.

Next, we will mark up the content for the modal body.

```
<div class="modal-body">
<label>Name</label><input type="text" ng-model="newUser.name"/>
<label>Subscription Type</label><input type="text" ng-model="newUser.
userType"/>
<label>Loyalty Score</label><input type="number" ng-model="newUser.
loyalty"/>
<label>Date of Joining</label><input type="date" ng-model="newUser.
joinDate"/>
<br/>
<button class="btn btn-success" ng-click="saveNewUser()"> Save User</
button>

</div>
```

The code is straightforward; we wrap our form elements within a <div> with the .modal-body class.

We have four form elements, which are tied to the respective properties of the newUser object.

The **Add New User** button, when clicked on, will call the AddNewUser function.

Note the type attributes for each of the input elements. These type attributes are automatically used by modern browsers for validations. AngularJS too appends its own CSS class to enable real-time validation notifications.

Next, we will add the code to our app/scripts/controllers/subscribers.js file.

The modal window makes use of the $modal service, so we will need to add it to SubscribersCtrl as highlighted in the following lines of code:

```
angular.module('hlApp')
    .controller('SubscribersCtrl', function ($scope,$http, $modal) {
```

Next, we will write the code to call the modal window.

As the Add New User button function will call the showModal function when clicked on, we will define that function at the end, just above the closing braces of our SubscribersCtrl controller as follows:

```
$scope.showModal=function () {
$scope.newUser={};
    var modalInstance = $modal.open({
        templateUrl: 'views/add-user.html'})}
```

The $modal service has a method named open(), with a couple of options, templateUrl being one of them.

We are also creating an empty model object named newUser. We will be using this to store the form data from the modal window.

Save the file and test it in the browser. Clicking on the **Add New User** Button should slide the modal window into view. However, this is quite static, and neither the close button nor the **Save User** buttons will work because we haven't yet coded in the saveNewUser() or cancel() functions.

An important thing to note is that the $modal service will create its own scope within the parent scope.

Another option that the $modal.open method supports is the controller that allows you to assign another controller, that binds to the view within the modal. Let us now add the controller option to modalInstance.

```
$scope.showModal= function () {
    var modalInstance = $modal.open({
        templateUrl: 'views/add-user.html',
        controller:'AddNewUserCtrl'

    })}
```

Next, we'll create AddNewUserCtrl within the same app/scripts/controllers/subscribers.js file.

We add this controller right at the end of the file after the `SubscribersCtrl` function ends as follows:

```
.controller('AddNewUserCtrl', function ($scope, $modalInstance) {
});
```

 Don't forget to remove the semicolon at the end of the `SubscribersCtrl` function.

Now, within `AddNewUserCtrl`, we'll define the functions for the **Cancel** button as follows:

```
.controller('AddNewUserCtrl', function ($scope, $modalInstance) {
  $scope.cancel =function(){
    $modalInstance.dismiss('cancel');
  };
});
```

Save the files and check to see if the **Add New User** and the **Cancel** buttons are working. Add the following CSS class to get your form to look aligned:

```
.modal-body input{
display:block;
}
```

You should be seeing something like the following screenshot:

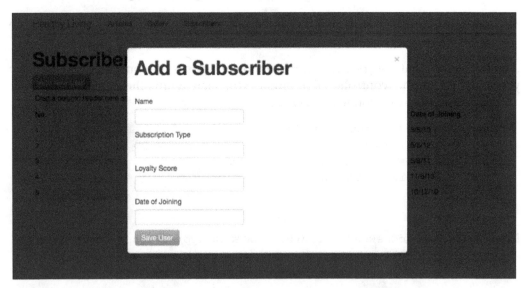

Now, let's add the rest of the code to save the user.

In the `AddNewUserCtrl` controller, add the following highlighted code:

```
.controller('AddNewUserCtrl', function ($scope,
$modalInstance, newUser) {
$scope.newUser=newUser;
$scope.saveNewUser=function(){
  $modalInstance.close(newUser);
};

  $scope.cancel =function(){
    $modalInstance.dismiss('cancel');
  }

});
```

We'll now add the last option to our `$modal.open` method, which is named `resolve`. The code is highlighted as shown in the following lines of code:

```
var modalInstance = $modal.open({
templateUrl: 'views/add-user.html',
controller: 'AddUserCtrl',
resolve: {
  newUser: function () {
  return $scope.newUser;
      }
    }
  });
```

Like most services, `$modal` also makes use of promises to return the objects and variables that have been asked for.

Here, in the `resolve` part, we are returning the `newUser` model object.

Now that we have the `newUser` model returned to us as a response to the promise, we need push the data from it into our `subscribers` model. This is done by the following piece of code:

```
modalInstance.result.then(function (selectedItem) {
$scope.subscribers.push({
no:$scope.subscribers.length+1,
name:$scope.newUser.name,
userType:$scope.newUser.userType,
loyalty:$scope.newUser.loyalty,
joinDate:$scope.newUser.joinDate

  });
});
```

Notice that for the no column, I'm simply taking the length of our current model and incrementing it by 1.

Also note that the preceding code is written within the showModal function.

The complete code for showModal should be as follows:

```
$scope.showModal=function () {
    $scope.newUser={};
    var modalInstance = $modal.open({
        templateUrl: 'views/add-user.html',
        controller:'AddNewUserCtrl',
        resolve: {
            newUser: function () {
            return $scope.newUser;
            }
        }

    })

    modalInstance.result.then(function (selectedItem) {
    $scope.subscribers.push({
    no:$scope.subscribers.length+1,
    name:$scope.newUser.name,
    userType:$scope.newUser.userType,
    loyalty:$scope.newUser.loyalty,
    joinDate:$scope.newUser.joinDate

        });
    });

}
```

Real-time form validations

Based on the type attribute of your input fields, AngularJS is adding the ng-valid and ng-invalid classes in real time. We can take advantage of this to give constructive feedback to the user.

What we will do is, if the entered text is valid, the text box will have a green border, and if the data in the text box is invalid, it will have a red border.

To achieve this, we will add the following CSS properties for these classes in the app/styles/main.css file:

```
.ng-valid{
    border: thin solid #090;
}
```

```
.ng-invalid{
    border: thin solid #990000;
}
```

With this, we complete our exercise of creating the clickable prototype.

In conclusion the following are a couple of reasons why building clickable prototypes in AngularJS is a good idea:

- It gives a clear picture to all the stakeholders on how the application is going to look and work.

- One can get valuable usability feedback and easily identify any usability issues by simply playing around with the prototype.

- The Presentation Layer code is production-ready, and during the actual time of development, we only need to swap the static data models with dynamic ones from web services. This will significantly cut down the development time.

- The time taken to build the click flows in AngularJS is much lesser than it would take if done using the regular HTML, CSS, and jQuery. Using regular HTML and CSS would also generate quite a bit of throw-away code, which isn't very efficient.

Summary

In this chapter, we saw how to keep the data separate from the presentation layer. I'm sure you also appreciated how we had to write very few lines of code to build the entire application.

We used Yeoman to scaffold our app and create the new pages that we wanted. We used the custom directives from Angular Bootstrap for the various components that we used across the application.

We also saw how routes work and how views and controllers are bound to a path using `routeProvider`.

We took advantage of Bootstrap's grid system and the predefined classes to build the entire website without having to write any large amounts of custom CSS code.

In the next chapter, we'll see how to build a fully functional application by integrating our frontend with a backed REST web service.

4
Using REST Web Services in Your AngularJS App

In the previous chapter, we saw how to build an application prototype using static data models.

During the actual development, we would obviously like to work with live dynamic data and would need it to be tied to a backend. In AngularJS, the easiest and most common way of interacting with backend application is via **Representational State Transfer (REST)** web services, using **JavaScript Object Notations (JSON)** formats.

In this chapter, we will see how to build an app that will display the latest box office movies for a selected country. We will make use of the easy-to-use web service APIs from www.rottentomatoes.com.

Some of the things that we will learn in this chapter are as follows:

- What are factories, services, and providers in AngularJS, and how they differ from each other
- How to make calls to a web service using the `$http` service
- How **Dependency Injection (DI)** works
- Understand how asynchronous calls are made and the concept of promises

Understanding the response from a REST API

Before we get started with building our application, let's quickly see how a RESTful web service works.

For this exercise, we will use the web service from the following link:

```
developer.rottentomatoes.com
```

You will need to create an API key to be able to use these services. So, go ahead, sign up, and register for an API key.

Feel free to go through the documentation to understand the different web services they provide and different types of parameters you need to pass.

We'll use the Box Office API to get the list of the latest box office movies. The URL for the API is as follows:

```
http://api.rottentomatoes.com/api/public/v1.0/lists/movies/
  box_office.json
```

To this, we need to pass the following additional parameters:

- **apikey**: The API key that you received when you signed up and registered an application
- **limit**: The maximum number of results you want the web service to return
- **country**: The country code for the country you'd like to see the results for

> The complete list of Rotten Tomatoes web services and the various parameters that each of them takes is neatly documented as follows:
>
> ```
> http://developer.rottentomatoes.com/docs
> ```

Like most RESTful web services, these parameters are simply appended to the URL as query strings. The final URL will look like the following one:

```
http://api.rottentomatoes.com/api/public/v1.0/lists/movies/box_
office.json?limit=5&country=us&apikey=<your API Key>
```

Testing a RESTful web service

Testing or checking the response of a REST web service is very easy. All you need to do is copy and paste the web service URL in your browser, and you should be able to see the results printed out in the JSON format.

In our case, we will copy and paste the following URL in the browser:

```
http://api.rottentomatoes.com/api/public/v1.0/lists/movies/
    box_office.json?limit=5&country=us&apikey=<your API Key>
```

As this response is minified, it might be difficult to read through it. We can use either `http://www.jsbeautifier.org/` or `http://www.dirtymarkup.com/` to clean up your web service output, or you can also use browser-based add-ons such as the RESTClient for Firefox or Postman and Advanced REST Client for Google Chrome browsers to preview and test the APIs.

Your output might look something like the following screenshot:

The output as seen on http://www.jsbeautifier.org/

Now, let's start building our application.

Jump starting your app development with Angular Seed

In the previous examples, we have been using Yeoman to scaffold our application. For this exercise, we will use the `angular-seed` project as a skeleton, on which we will start building our application.

The `angular-seed` project is available on GitHub and is maintained by the core AngularJS Development team, so we can be assured that it is up to date.

Let's create a folder named `abo`, short for **Angular Box Office**, and download the forked `angular-seed` project from the following URL:

`https://github.com/areai51/angular-seed`

You can choose to either download the ZIP file or clone it using Git and by typing in the following command in the terminal:

git clone https://github.com/areai51/angular-seed.git

> The original `angular-seed` project on the GitHub project, which is at `https://github.com/angular/angular-seed`, is constantly evolving with minor changes being committed in all the time. We use the preceding forked version to ensure that the code base is relevant to the chapters of this book.

Files and folders in Angular Seed

Once you have downloaded the files and extracted them to your `abo` folder, run the following command, from within the `abo` folder, in the terminal:

npm install

This will install the devdependencies mentioned in our `package.json` file, and it will also run the `bower install` command and automatically install the bower components defined in our `bower.json` file.

Adding Bootstrap libraries

As we want to make our application look good and don't want to spend time writing our CSS styles from scratch, we'll use the **Content Delivery Network (CDN)** version of a **Bootswatch** theme. Bootswatch is a collection of custom themes built using the Bootstrap framework. The site, `http://www.bootstrapcdn.com/`, hosts CDN versions of Bootstrap and Bootswatch CSS files.

For this particular exercise, we'll use the **Simplex** theme and the CDN URL, which is as follows:

`//netdna.bootstrapcdn.com/bootswatch/3.0.0/simplex/bootstrap.min.css`

Let's open our `index.html` file and include the CSS file for the Simplex theme as highlighted in the following code:

```
<head>
  <meta charset="utf-8">
  <title>My AngularJS App</title>

  <link rel="stylesheet" href="//netdna.bootstrapcdn.com/bootswatch/
    3.0.0/simplex/bootstrap.min.css"/>
  <link rel="stylesheet" href="css/app.css"/>
</head>
```

> Make sure that you are including the `simplex` CSS file above the `app.css` file; this will allow us to override any of the default classes by writing them in the `app.css` file.

Starting your Node web server

Now, in most cases, you should be able to view your application by simply running the `index.html` file from the filesystem. However, in many cases, you would need to run it from within a web server. You can deploy the files in the public root folder of any web server, or you can run the standalone Node server script that comes as a part of Angular Seed.

To start your Node web server, run the following command:

npm start

This will start the web server on `http://localhost:8000`; you will be able to access your `index.html` file at the following URL:

`http://localhost:8000/app/index.html`

You should be seeing the page styled with the Simplex theme. Now that we have everything ready, let's start coding our app.

Mark-up our Layout

We'll start by adding some basic layout code to the `app/index.html` file located in the root of our application folder.

Replace the current HTML code within the `<body>` tags with the following code. Leave the following `<script>` tags at the bottom intact as they are:

```html
<div class="container">
  <div class="col-md-12 text-center">
    <a href="#" class="brand ">Angular Box Office</a>
  </div>
  <hr>
  <div ng-view></div>
</div>
```

We are wrapping `ng-view` with the default Bootstrap wrapper container and adding in the code for our brand name. The container class would get our page contents to the center of the screen. The `col-md-12` class will create a `<div>` element that is 12-column wide; it is the equivalent of `.span12` in bootstrap2. The `text-center` attribute is used to center align the text. The brand class is added so that we can style the brand name.

Creating the routes

Let's replace the current stock routes with more meaningful ones. Update the `app/js/app.js` file by adding the highlighted lines of code:

```javascript
'use strict';
// Declare app level module which depends on filters,
  and services
angular.module('myApp', [
  'ngRoute',
  'myApp.filters',
  'myApp.services',
  'myApp.directives',
  'myApp.controllers'
]).
config(['$routeProvider', function($routeProvider) {
  $routeProvider.when('/', {templateUrl: 'partials/movie-list.html',
    controller: 'MovieListCtrl'});
  $routeProvider.otherwise({redirectTo: '/'});
}]);
```

For this application, we'll need only one route and one partial. So, we set / to point to `partials/movie-list.html` and map it to the `MovieListCtrl` controller.

 Don't forget to rename or create your `movie-list.html` file in the `partials` folder.

Understanding AngularJS services

When you are building medium to large-scale applications where certain functionalities are common across different pages or sections, then instead of repeating the same piece of code within every controller, it's best to write it within a service and call it within the different components.

A classic example would be getting the list of products from a backend web service. The code to make the web service call, passing in the authentication tokens or API keys, getting the response back, and parsing the response can all be put into a service. This service can then be called from the various controllers, directives, or other components that need to display the product list.

A couple of points to remember with regard to services are as follows:

- They are singleton objects that are initiated only once, and they persist throughout the lifetime of the app
- Services are lazy loaded, that is, they get initiated only when an application component depends on it
- These services are "injected" or mapped to the components using DI

AngularJS comes with several built-in services such as `$animate`, `$log`, `$http`, `$sanitize`, and so on. A list of all of the available AngularJS services can be viewed at `https://code.angularjs.org/1.2.18/docs/api/ng/service`.

Besides these ready-to-use services, we can also create our own service.

The `$provide` service exposes numerous methods that can be used to create and register our service, and they are as follows:

- `provider()`: This is used to register a provider function with the `$injector` function. Provider functions are constructor functions. They can contain additional methods that allow the provider to be configured.
- `service()`: This is used to register an instance of the service using a constructor function. The constructor is invoked using `new` to create an instance of the service.

- `factory()`: This is used to register a service factory. It is one of the easiest and most widely used methods to use a service. It can return a primitive value, a function, or an object.

- `value()`: This is used to register a service where the output returned is either a string, number, array, function, or object. Values can only be accessed by services.

- `constant()`: This is used to register a constant service and is exactly similar to the value service, the only difference being that constants can be accessed by both services and providers.

Writing your first factory service

As we learned earlier, a factory is written to return a single object, array, or function that can then be passed as a parameter to any other function or controller, across the entire application.

Let's create a factory function to store a country list and pass it on to our models via the controller.

Let's open the `app/js/services.js` file and add the following code:

```
'use strict';
angular.module('myApp.services', []).
value('version', '0.1')

.factory('rtmFactory', function() {
    var countries = [
    {name: 'USA',code: 'us'},
    {name: 'UK',code: 'uk'},
    {name: 'France',code: 'fr'}
    ];
    return {
        getCountries: function() {
            return countries;
        }
    }
})
```

Here, we are creating a factory named `rtmFactory` and chaining it to the `myApp` module.

Don't forget to remove the semicolon after the line, `value` (`'version'`, `'0.1'`), so that the factory can be chained to it.

Within this factory, we will create an object to store the list of countries and their country code. We will use this data to view the box office movies for the different countries.

Next, create a function named `getCountries` that will return the countries' object when called.

Before we go about getting our country data into the controller, let's pause to briefly understand DI, which we will be using more often from now on.

Dependency Injection

Dependency Injection is a software design pattern where one or more dependencies are injected or passed to an object as a reference. This allows us to load code only when needed.

 You can read more about DI at `https://code.angularjs.org/1.2.18/docs/guide/di`.

In our example, we have our factory that contains a data object, and we pass it into our controller using DI.

AngularJS has a `$injector` service that is responsible for doing the job of looking up the services and injecting them into the functions.

There are multiple ways of injecting dependencies into a function in AngularJS, the easiest being simply passing the dependencies as parameters of the function within which it's needed.

We will now pass our `rtmFactory` service to our `MovieListCtrl` controller as a parameter.

Let's open the `app/js/controllers.js` file and update the code as follows:

```
'use strict';
angular.module('myApp.controllers', []).
controller('MovieListCtrl', ['$scope', 'rtmFactory',
    function($scope, rtmFactory) {
        $scope.countries = rtmFactory.getCountries();
    }
])
```

Coding the partial

Let's markup the partial and ascertain that the data returned from the factory is visible on the frontend page.

Add the following code to the `app/partials/movie-list.html` file:

```
<h1>Box Office Movies</h1>
<button class="btn btn-info" ng-repeat="country in countries">
{{country.name}}</button>
```

We simply run `ng-repeat` to loop the buttons. The `btn` and `btn-info` classes are used to style the button.

Save the files and view the application at `http://localhost:8000/app/index.html`. Make sure that you have the Node server running.

If you get to see the three buttons with the country names displayed, that means everything is working great, and we are all set for more meaningful stuff.

If you don't get to see those three buttons, fire up your console to see if there are any errors and fix them.

 Use the excellent Firebug add-on for Firefox or the Developer Tools in Google Chrome or Internet Explorer to check error stack in the console.

Calling the REST web service using $http

The `$http` service is a built-in AngularJS service that is used to allow the AngularJS app to talk to backend systems or other third-party systems using web services. The `$http` service is essentially a wrapper for the browser's `XMLHttpRequest` object and allows us to work at ease without having to worry about the low-level APIs.

The `$http` service function accepts a configuration object as an argument and returns a promise with two methods: `success` and `error`. We can use the `.then()` method to register callbacks, which in turn returns the response as a single object.

The basic usage of the `$http` service would look like the following lines of code:

```
$http({
    method: 'GET',
    url: 'api/api-endpoint'
}).success(function(data, status, headers, config) {
    // called on success
```

```
}).error(function(data, status, headers, config) {
    //called on error
})
```

The preceding code can also be written using shortcut methods and would look like the following lines of code:

```
$http.get('api/api-endpoint').success(successCallback).
    error(errorCallback)
```

Similar to `.get()`, the following additional shortcut methods are available as part of the $http service.

- `$http.head`
- `$http.post`
- `$http.jsonp`
- `$http.put`
- `$http.delete`

Now, we'll write our factory function to make a call to the Rotten Tomatoes API and return the JSON response.

From the API documentation, we know that the endpoint for the web service is as follows:

```
http://api.rottentomatoes.com/api/public/v1.0/lists/movies/
    box_office.json?limit=10&country='us'&callback=JSON_CALLBACK&apikey
    =<api-key>
```

We need to pass our API key and the country code along with the limits as a query string. It will then respond with a JSON response that contains details of the movies.

We first register our API key as a constant within our `app/js/services.js` file as follows:

```
.constant('API_KEY','<Enter your api key>')
```

Then, we will create our `getMovies` function as highlighted in the following `app/js/services.js` file:

```
'use strict';
angular.module('myApp.services', []).
value('version', '0.1')
.constant('API_KEY','<Enter your api key>')
```

```
.factory('rtmFactory', function() {
    var countries = [
    {name: 'USA',code: 'us'},
    {name: 'UK',code: 'uk'},
    {name: 'France',code: 'fr'}
    ];
    return {
        getCountries: function() {
            return countries;
        },
        getMovies:function(countryCode){
        var key='';
        return $http.jsonp('http://api.rottentomatoes.com/api/
          public/v1.0/lists/movies/box_office.json?limit
            =10&country='+countryCode+'&callback=JSON_CALLBACK&
              apikey='+API_KEY);
    }

    };
});
```

As you can see from the highlighted code, the `getMovies` function accepts one parameter for the country code, which will then be used to build our API URL.

Also, notice that we are making use of the `$http.jsonp` method instead of the regular `$http.get` method to make our web service call. This is to overcome the same-origin policy in browsers.

JSONP, which stands for **JSON with padding**, is one of the ways of getting content from another domain by leveraging the property of the `<script>` tag.

As there is a dependency on the `$http` and `API_KEY` service, we need to inject it into our factory function as a parameter, which we have done as follows:

```
.factory('rtmFactory', ['$http', 'API_KEY',function($http,API_KEY){
}])
```

That completes our work in the `services.js` file. Let's see how to add this to our controller and also understand the concept of promises.

Using promise for asynchronous calls

We know that services are always lazily loaded and are executed asynchronously. Two ways to deal with such asynchronous calls are using callbacks and promises.

While callbacks are OK when making individual requests, they tend to get messy when you need to do nested callbacks. This is where promises come in handy, as they can be easily chained.

As per the proposal at CommonJS, "**Promises** provide a well-defined interface for interacting with an object that represents the result of an action that is performed asynchronously, and may or may not be finished at any given point in time."

Promises in AngularJS are implemented via the `$q` service, which is based on the Q Library by Kris Kowal. It is available at `https://github.com/kriskowal/q`.

There are two components to this: Deferred and Promise. The Deferred object is used to notify the status of the task. The Promise object provides the result of the deferred task.

The Deferred object has three methods: `resolve()`, `reject()`, and `notify()`. The Promise object also has three methods: `then()`, `catch()`, and `finally()`. You can read more about the `$q` service and these methods at `https://docs.angularjs.org/api/ng/service/$q`.

Of the three methods of the Promise object, the `.then()` method is the most important one and is also a part of the proposed specs at CommonJS. The syntax to use the `.then()` method is as follows:

```
.then(successCallback, errorCallBack, notificationCallBack)
```

Once the result is available, the `then()` method will call either `successCallBack` or `errorCallBack`. The `notificationCallBack` method might be called multiple times while the promise is being resolved or rejected and is used to provide an indication of the progress.

Let's now see how to use promises in our controller. Open the `app/js/controllers.js` file and add the following code in the `MovieListCtrl` function:

```
$scope.loadMovies = function(countryCode) {
    rtmFactory.getMovies(countryCode).then(
        function(response) {

            var movieArray = response.data.movies;
            console.log(JSON.stringify(movieArray))
            $scope.movies = movieArray;

        },
        function(response) {
            // error message
```

```
        }
    )
};

    $scope.loadMovies('us');
```

To ensure modularity and reusability, we wrap our code within a `loadMovie` function that accepts `countryCode` as an input parameter, which is further passed down to the `getMovies` factory function.

Then, we chain our promise to it using `.then()` and write our success callback function, where we trim our response from the web service and store it in an array that is then returned back.

In the error callback function, we will display a suitable error message.

In the last line, we invoke the `loadMovies` function that passes `us` as the default country code.

This completes our work in the controller. Next, we will write the code for our view.

Displaying data from the JSON response

Now is the time to mark up the views to display the parsed data from our JSON output.

Let's open `app/partials/movie-list.html` and add the markup as follows:

```html
<div class="pin-layout">
  <div ng-repeat="movie in movies">
    <div class="thumbnail">
        <h3 class="caption">{{movie.title}}</h3>
      <img width="180" ng-src="{{movie.posters.detailed}}"
        alt="{{movie.title}}">
        <p>{{movie.synopsis}}</p>
    </div>
  </div>
</div>
```

This piece of code should be self-explanatory by now.

We have a wrapper div with a class named `pin-layout`; within it, we call another div with `ng-repeat` that will loop through each record of the movie model.

Within this, we will be displaying the movie title, poster image, and the critics' comments.

In case you would like to display additional data, you can do so by simply displaying the appropriate property name within the {{ }} brackets.

 Refer to the *Testing a RESTful Web Service* section of this chapter to see how you can view the JSON response to understand the various attributes that are available.

Save the file and refresh it in the browser to see the movies' data load in.

Unit testing our application

The `angular-seed` project comes with Unit testing baked in. In the terminal window, run the following command:

npm test

This will run the default tests and show the output in the terminal window. We will notice that the tests fail. The reason being our tests are looking for the `myCtrl1` or `myCtrl2` function within our controller, but it isn't there.

Let's open up our `test/unit/controllersSpec.js` file and remove those default tests. Save the file and immediately you will notice that our tests pass.

Let's write our Unit test to test the web services we wrote.

Mocking $http during Unit testing

Unit tests are meant to test the pieces of code we have written. They are not expected to verify the responses from external systems. Hence, in situations where our code needs to make external requests, we simply fake the request and respond with a canned response. This is called mocking, and in our case, we will use the `$httpBackend` service to mock our `$http` requests.

We start by replacing the code in the `test/unit/servicesSpec.js` file with the following lines of code:

```
'use strict';
describe('service', function() {
  beforeEach(module('myApp.services'));
  describe('rtmFactory', function() {

  })
})
```

Now, within the `rtmfactory` function, we will declare some objects and create our function that we would like to be injected before every test.

Continue by adding the following code to the same function:

```
var scope, httpBackend, rtmFactory, result;
beforeEach(inject(function(_rtmFactory_, $httpBackend) {
    httpBackend = $httpBackend;
    rtmFactory = _rtmFactory_

    var url = "http://api.rottentomatoes.com/api/public/v1.0/
lists/movies/box_office.json?limit=10&country=us&callback=JSON_
CALLBACK&apikey<api_key>"

    var mockedResponse = [
    {"id": "12312312","title": "Transformers"},
    {"id": "445433","title": "Mackenna's Gold"},
    {"id": "3335","title": "Star Wars"}
    ]

    httpBackend.when("JSONP", url).respond(mockedResponse)
}))
```

Don't forget to replace `<api_key>` with the actual `api_key` value in the `url` variable.

As you can see, we injected the function with `_rtmFactory_` and `httpBackend` services as dependencies.

Next, we define the URL for our web service and the mocked response that it should return. The `$httpBackend` service supports two methods to specify how the mocked data is returned:

- `$httpBackend.expect()`: This is used to make assertions on the request made by the application and will return the response for those particular requests. The order of the requests is also important here.

- `$httpBackend.when()`: This is used when we need to simply specify a backend definition. This will return the canned response as long as the request was made.

In our case, we use the `$httpBackend.when()` method to set our response.

Once this is done, we continue to write our Unit test as follows:

```
it('should contain three items', function() {
    var wsRequest = rtmFactory.getMovies('us')
    wsRequest.then(function(data) {
```

```
        result = data.data.length
    })
    httpBackend.flush()
    expect(result).toEqual(3)
});
```

We write this unit test within the `rtmFactory` suite description after the `beforeEach` method.

Here, we make the request to the `getMovies` method in our `rtmfFactory` service, and making use of the promise, we store the length of our returned object.

In the final step, we verify that the length of the result is 3.

Save the file and switch to the terminal window. Karma would have detected the change in the file and would have automatically run the tests again. This time, you should be seeing all greens with a success message.

Go ahead and write a couple of Unit tests.

Creating a Pinterest style layout

We now have a functional app, but it's nowhere close to looking good. So, let's add some CSS styles to give it that neat finish.

The class named `pin-layout` was there for a purpose. We are going to create a Pinterest-style layout to display our box office movies.

To do this, we make use of the CSS3 property called `column-count`, which automatically converts your data into a multicolumn layout.

Let's open our `app/css/app.css` file and add the following CSS classes:

```css
.pin-layout{
        column-count: 4;
        column-gap: 0px;
        -moz-column-count: 4;
        -moz-column-gap: 0px;
        -webkit-column-count: 4;
        -webkit-column-gap: 0px;
}
```

The preceding code sets the column count to 4 and the gap between two columns to 0.

 The column-count and column-gap properties are supported in IE10 and Opera, We use browser prefixes such as -moz and -webkit to get it to work in Firefox, and Chrome and Safari respectively.

Save the file and test it on the browser to see the data flow within the four columns.

While this is nice, there are a couple of issues. For one, everything is sticking to each other, and two, some of the data towards the bottom of the page is split and flows into the next column. Ideally, we would like each movie block to be contained within a single box, such as index cards.

To fix this, let's style the thumbnail class by adding the following CSS code:

```
.thumbnail{
    display: inline-block;
    margin:5px;
    padding:5px;
    border-radius: 5px;
    box-shadow: 2px 2px 5px #ccc;
    background: #fff;
}
```

The most important property here is display: inline-block. It ensures that the content within a thumbnail doesn't autoflow into the next column.

The rest of the CSS is to make it visually appealing. We add a margin and padding to give it some spacing around the borders; we add a border radius of 5 to give it those nice rounded corners and a box shadow for some highlights.

While we are working on the CSS file, let's also quickly add properties to style our brand logo by adding the following CSS properties:

```
.brand{
  color:#ff6600;
  font-size: 50px;
  font-family: georgia;
}
```

Save the files and check the browser; your page should be looking like the following screenshot:

Adding actions to the buttons

Now, let's add some click events to our button so that clicking on them shows the box office movies for the respective country.

For this, let's open our movie-list partial located at `app/partials/movie-list.html` and tweak the code for the buttons as follows:

```
<button class="btn btn-info" ng-click="loadMovies(country.code)"
    ng-repeat="country in countries"> {{country.name}}</button>
```

All we do is add the `ng-click` directive and call the `loadMovie` function, passing the country code that we receive from our model. This is all that is needed to get the buttons functional.

Save your file, and refresh your browser to enjoy your finished application.

Summary

This completes our exercise of building our AngularJS Box Office app.

We can add some more features such as showing a "View Details" link, which would directly take us to the "Movie Details" page on www.imdb.com.

We can do this by passing the IMDB ID available within our JSON response and pass it to the following URL:

```
http://www.imdb.com/title/tt<imdb-id>.
```

During this exercise, we learned about factories and how to make calls to a web service from within a factory. We also learned about the factory's asynchronous calls and how Promises are used to return the values whenever an asynchronous function has finished processing.

Finally, we finished off by styling our application to make it look like a Pinterest board.

In the next chapter, we will see how to create a Facebook app that will work as a friend's birthday reminder.

5
Facebook Friends' Birthday Reminder App

It's time to build our very own Facebook Friends' Birthday Reminder app folks!

In the previous chapter, we saw how to consume a REST web service and display the data that we received from a web service using a factory. We learned about promises and why they are important while making asynchronous calls via factories.

Building on this, we will now see how to build an app that will consume Facebook's open graph, **Application Programming Interface (API)**, to display your friends' upcoming birthdays.

We will also be learning about AngularJS directives, and build our very first directive to implement Facebook's authentication.

Before you proceed, make sure you are comfortable with the following features of AngularJS:

- Routes
- Controllers and Partials
- The concept of promise

You are also going to need to have a Facebook account with some friends in it who have agreed to share information with your app

Understanding the Facebook SDK

Facebook provides a **Software Development Kit (SDK)** for using the Facebook APIs in various platforms and languages. It has a wealth of information, sample codes, and "How-tos" to help you get started quickly with integrating Facebook into your application.

All this information is available at `https://developers.facebook.com/`.

Since we will be building a web application, we would be more interested in the JavaScript SDK available at `https://developers.facebook.com/docs/web/`.

The Social Graph

The **Social Graph** is a mapping of different people and how they are related to each other within a network. Facebook uses this term to refer to the Facebook platform, which was introduced in May 2007. Within the Facebook Social Graph context, every person, page, photo, or comment is a node that is connected to each other with the relations they share.

The Graph API

The Graph API is the primary way of interfacing with Facebook's Social Graph. The Graph API is a set of REST-based web services, using which you can query for the information you need, post information, upload videos, and so on.

The complete guide to using the Graph API can be found at `https://developers.facebook.com/docs/graph-api/using-graph-api/`.

The Graph API Explorer

The Graph API Explorer is an excellent tool to explore Facebook's Graph APIs. It allows you to build and test your web service requests and view the output in real time. The following screenshot shows the **Graph API Explorer** window:

The **Graph API Explorer** window

The Graph API Explorer can be accessed at `https://developers.`
`facebook.com/tools/explorer`.

To view the response of a Graph API, type the parameters in the Graph API textbox
and hit the **Submit** button.

Some examples that you can try out quickly are given in the following table:

Graph API URL	Description
/me	This will display the logged-in user's profile information.
/4	This will display the public profile of the user whose user ID is 4, which in this case happens to be that of Mark Zuckerberg.
/me/friends	This will display the list of all my friends who have agreed to share information with your app

Graph API URL	Description
`/me/friends?fields=gender, name,devices`	This will display the list of friends along with their gender and also the devices they use to access Facebook.
`/102452128776?fields=app_ name,weekly_active_ users,name`	This will display the name and weekly active users of the Farmville app whose app ID is `102452128776`.
`michaeljackson?fields=like s,name`	Instead of using IDs, one can also use the username in the API search. This, for example, will give us the number of likes for Michael Jackson's page.

To view the list of all the fields or "edges" as Facebook calls it, use the **+** sign on the left panel, which will open up the popup that lists out all the fields that are available for the current web service.

 It is strongly recommended that you first formulate your API request parameters on the Graph API Explorer and then use it in your application.

Creating your Facebook app

To use the Graph API in our web application, you will need an app ID, which means we'll need to create a Facebook app. This section walks you through the process of creating a Facebook app:

1. Visit the Facebook Developer section at `https://developers.facebook. com/`, and click on the **Apps** link on the navigation bar on the top. Make sure you are registered as a developer.

2. Select the **Create New App** button on the **Apps** dropdown.

3. On the popup that appears, fill in the name for your app; `Birthday Reminder` would be a good choice.

4. Continue through the steps by answering the Captcha and completing the process of your app creation.

5. The next step is to let Facebook know the URL where you are going to host the web application. We do this on the **Settings** page. For this chapter, we will be running our application from `http://localhost:8000`, so let's put that into the site URL's textbox, and hit **Save** at the bottom of the page.

This completes the process of setting up our Facebook app for our application. Once your app has been created, please note down the app ID as we will need to use that in our application. The app ID can be found on the Facebook apps summary page that is shown in the following screenshot:

Setting up our project

We are now ready to get started with building our `Birthday Reminder` application. We'll use the `angular-seed` project to help us quickly get started.

Let's create our project folder named `birthday-reminder` and download the fork of the `angular-seed` project from `https://github.com/areai51/angular-seed`. Feel free to download the ZIP file and extract it, or clone the Git repository into the `birthday-reminder` folder. Then, run `npm install` in the terminal to download and install the dependencies required for this project.

Running your application

In case you already have a web server such as Apache, IIS, or Nginx running, then you can place the `birthday-reminder` folder in your web root, or create a sym link to the folder and run it via `localhost`.

The `angular-seed` project also comes with its own web server. To start the web server, first make sure you are in the `birthday-reminder` folder, and then run the following commands in the terminal:

```
npm install
```

```
npm start
```

This will start the node server at `http://localhost:8000`. Navigate into the app and then click on the `index.html` file to view our running AngularJS app. What we see now is obviously the default skeleton that comes as a part of the `angular-seed` project.

Delving into AngularJS directives

Before we get started with building our application and integrating Facebook and all, let's first take a moment to learn about directives as we plan to integrate our Facebook authentication module as a directive.

What is a directive?

A **directive** is a marker on a DOM element that tells AngularJS to transform the DOM element or attach a specified behavior to it. The marker would be a CSS class, a custom attribute, or a custom element name.

AngularJS comes with a large set of predefined directives, many of which we've already been using till now. Some of the built-in directives that we've used so far are ng-app, ng-repeat, ng-model, and ng-view.

One of the coolest features of AngularJS is the ability to create your own custom directives that can be created once and used multiple times within your application.

Importance of naming conventions for directives

Directives need to follow a strict naming convention for them to work properly. This is because AngularJS normalizes the element names or attribute names to match it to the directive.

As a rule, directive names in JavaScript must follow the **camelCase** naming convention, while in HTML, they need to be hyphenated. For example, in JavaScript, if you name your directive as myDirective, then in HTML, you'll need to call it my-directive.

The anatomy of a directive

An AngularJS directive along with its most commonly-used options would look like the following code snippet:

```
.directive('myDirective',function(){
  return{
    restrict: 'AE',
    transclude: true,
    scope: {},
    link: function(scope,element,attrs){},
    template:" ",
```

```
    templateUrl: " ",
    controller:function(){}
  }
});
```

As you can see in the preceding code, we are calling our directive `myDirective`.

Next, the `return` function is essentially a factory function that is responsible for creating the directive. It returns an object with various options such as `restrict`, `transclude`, `scope`, and so on.

Let's look at what each of those options mean.

Option	Description
restrict	This defines whether the directive can be used as an attribute or element. Setting it to E would mean that the directive can be used only as an element. Setting it to AE means you can use it either as an element or attribute. The default setting is to use it as an attribute.
transclude	Setting `transclude` to `true` will allow the directive to gain access to the parent scope over that of its own internal isolated scope.
scope	The `scope` option is used to create an isolated scope where we can pass parameters, as attribute values, to a directive.
link	The `link` option is used when you would like to modify the DOM. The `link` option takes a function that has three parameters: `scope`, `element`, and `attribute`; their description is as follows: • scope: This is the AngularJS scope within the directive • `element`: This is the element name that the directive maps to • `attribute`: This is the attribute names along with their values
template	The `template` option accepts an HTML string that is injected into the DOM where the directive is called. This is ideal when you need to display about one line of content.
templateUrl	When we have a lot of content that needs to be displayed, then it's best to create a separate HTML file and call it into the directive using the `templateUrl` option. This is also the recommended way of loading the template within the directive.
controller	We can define the controller functions in a directive, just like how we use a regular controller. This controller will get bound to the template of the directive.

At a higher level, both `link` and `controller` do the same thing, the main difference is that `controller` can expose an API while `link` will interact with the controller.

Writing our first directive

Let's start by writing a very basic directive. Navigate to and open the `app/js/ directives.js` file and add in the following highlighted code:

```
'use strict';

angular.module('myApp.directives', []).
    directive('appVersion', ['version', function(version) {
        return function(scope, elm, attrs) {
            elm.text(version);
        };
    }])
    .directive('myFacebook', [function(){
        return{
            link: function(scope,element,attributes){
                scope.username="John Doe"
            },
            template:"Welcome {{username}}"
        }
    }])
```

 Don't forget to replace the ";" with the "." after the first directive ends.

We are going to create a directive named `myFacebook`, and in the `link` option, we will set a `scope` variable named `username`. We will also set the `template` option to display the welcome message.

Now, we will call our directive in the `partials/partials1.html` file. Open the file and add the following line to the `partials1.html` file:

```
<div my-facebook></div>
```

As you can see here, in the preceding HTML line of code, we call the directive by using hyphens instead of the camelCase syntax.

While separating the two words using a hyphen is the most commonly-used approach, one can also call the directive `my:facebook` or `my_facebook`. To ensure that your HTML meets the W3C's validation criteria, you will need to use `data-my-facebook` or `x-data-my-facebook`.

Save your file and navigate to the browser URL `http://localhost:8000/ app/index.html#/view1` to see your directive in action. Make sure that the `Welcome{{username}}` template has correctly resolved to **Hello John Doe**.

Adding a Facebook login

Using the Facebook JavaScript SDK, we are going to create our very own directive for the Facebook login. We could simply copy and paste the sample Facebook login code available on the developer portal into our `index.html` file, and it would just work. However, this wouldn't be a clean approach. Instead, using directives helps to make the code abstract, thus keeping it clean, and once you have your own directive, it becomes quite easy to add the Facebook login into any of your other projects.

Now, let's try and get our Facebook login to work.

Adding the fb-root div element

Whenever we use the JavaScript SDK for Facebook, it's important that we have an empty `<div>` element with an ID named `fb-root` just after the `<body>` tag. The SDK uses this `<div>` element to insert other elements as needed.

Let's open up our `app/index.html` file and add the following highlighted `<div>` element:

```
<body>
    <div id="fb-root"></div>
```

In case you don't create the `<div>` element with ID `fb-root`, the SDK will also autocreate it while rendering the page.

Loading the Facebook SDK

Often, it is quite easy to call any custom JavaScript code, plugin, or authentication module in an AngularJS application by simply wrapping it into the directive's return function and calling the directive in the view.

Let's modify the code within our `myFacebook` directive to the following code snippet:

```
.directive('myFacebook', [
  function() {
    return {
      link: function(scope, element, attrs) {

        // Load the SDK asynchronously
        (function(d) {
          var js, id = 'facebook-jssdk',
            ref = d.getElementsByTagName('script')[0];
          if (d.getElementById(id)) {
            return;
```

```
        }
        js = d.createElement('script');
        js.id = id;
        js.async = true;
        js.src = "//connect.facebook.net/en_US/all.js";
        ref.parentNode.insertBefore(js, ref);
      }(document));

      // Initialize FB
      window.fbAsyncInit = function() {
        FB.init({
          appId: '248377671987957',
          status: true, // check login status
          cookie: true, // enable cookies to access the session
          xfbml: false // parse XFBML
        });

        //Check FB Status

        FB.getLoginStatus(function(response) {
          console.log(response);
        });

      };

      scope.username = "John Doe";
    },
    template: "Welcome {{username}}"
  };
  }
]);
```

The preceding code has been referenced from v 1.0 of the **Facebook Login Flow** sample code available at https://developers.facebook.com/docs/facebook-login/login-flow-for-web/v1.0.

 Facebook as recently made quite a few changes to Version 2.0 of their APIs, especially for the friends_* permission, This will impact all new apps being created. Read more about these changes at https://developers.facebook.com/docs/apps/changelog#v2_0_permissions.

As you can see, we are loading and initializing the Facebook SDK within the link function.

We first load the SDK asynchronously. This is important from a performance point of view so as to not block the loading of the other elements that are being loaded as a part of the page content. The window.fbAsyncInit method will execute as soon as the SDK files have been downloaded.

Next, we fire the FB.init call to initialize the FB object. This is where you need to define the app ID that you would have received at the time of creating the app on the Facebook developer portal. Refer to the *Creating your Facebook app* section to see how to get your app ID.

The FB.init call has the following four options:

Options	Description
appId	This is the app ID for the Facebook application you created on the Facebook developer portal.
status	Setting status to true will try to get the current user's status by using Oauth.
	Setting it to false would improve the page load time, but this would then require you to check the login status manually.
cookie	This needs to be set to true so that we allow the server to access the sessions.
xfbml	The SDK uses the xfbml: true setting to load social plugins if any. In this case, since we are not using any social plugins, we can set it to false.

Once the FB object is initialized, let's check the login status by looking at the response of the getLoginStatus function.

Let's refresh our page in the browser and look for the status response in the browser console. Depending on whether you are logged in or not and whether your app has the necessary permissions, we would get one of the following statuses:

Status	Description
status="unknown"	The user is not logged in to Facebook
status="not_authorized"	The user is logged in but hasn't authorized the app yet
status="connected"	The user is logged in and the app is authorized

In our case, we would get either of the first two responses.

To allow the user to log in and authorize the app, we'll need to call the
FB.login() function.

Let's do so by modifying our code in the getLoginStatus function by adding
the highlighted code:

```
FB.getLoginStatus(function(response) {
    if (response.status == 'connected') {
        FB.api('/me', function(response) {
            scope.username=response.name;
            console.log(scope.username);
                });
    } else {
        FB.login();
    }
});
```

Here, we check the login status, and if the status response is connected, we make
a request to the /me web service and get the name of the logged-in user. In case the
response status is not connected, we'll call the FB.login() function.

Save the file and refresh the page in the browser. On refreshing, you now get the
Facebook popup window asking the user to either log in or authorize the app.

 Make sure the browser is not blocking the Facebook popup.

Once you have logged in and have given the necessary permission to the app, you'll
need to refresh the page to notice the logged-in user's name displayed on the console.
As you see the correct name being displayed in the console, you'll notice that the
welcome message on the page continues to show **Welcome John Doe**. Ideally, this
should have changed because we are setting scope.username to the logged-in user's
name value.

The answer to why the value for scope.username did not change on the view page
even though it was updated in the console lies in understanding AngularJS's $watch
and $digest functions.

Understanding $watch and $digest

The two-way binding and the ability to update the content on a page without having
to refresh the entire page are some of the core features of AngularJS. AngularJS is
able to update the content instantaneously by making use of $watch and $digest.

AngularJS will set up a $watch function for every element in the scope object that is displayed on the page. All these $watch elements are stored in a watch list.

All events within the angular-context are automatically wrapped within a $apply function. It is this $apply function that forces a $digest loop to run each time an event is fired.

This $digest loop will iterate through each of the $watch functions in the $watch list and check to see if the value of the scope variable has changed, and in case it has changed, it would update the DOM to reflect the updated value. This is also known as **dirty checking**.

When to use $apply

The obvious question that arises is why didn't the username update in our view? The reason for that is two-fold:

- The Facebook SDK is loaded asynchronously, which means the value of scope.username is updated after the initial $digest loop has run.

- The value for scope.username is being set from outside of the angular-context. Due to this, it is not automatically wrapped within the $apply function, which in turn doesn't fire the $digest loop.

When you are setting values in a scope from external libraries/functions such as jQuery or the Facebook SDK like in our example, these are common problems.

The way to force AngularJS to fire the $digest loop is by manually wrapping the scope variables within the $apply function.

To make sure our views update the welcome message, let's wrap scope.username within the $apply function.

We'll make the changes in the app/directives.js file by adding the following highlighted code:

```
FB.getLoginStatus(function(response) {
  if (response.status == 'connected') {
    FB.api('/me', function(response) {

      scope.$apply(function() {
        scope.username = response.name;
      });
      console.log(scope.username);
    });
```

```
    } else {
      FB.login();
    }
  });
```

Save the files and refresh the page in the browser. You would initially see **John Doe**, but after a few seconds, it would get automatically updated to show the logged-in user's name.

Getting the user's friend list

Now that we know how to make requests to the Facebook API and get it to update correctly in our views, let's now see how to get the list of friends of the logged-in user.

We will create our function named `loadFriends` and call it within the `controller` option of the `myFriends` directive, as shown in the following code snippet:

```
controller: function($scope) {
  $scope.loadFriends = function() {

    FB.api('/me/friends', function(response) {
      $scope.$apply(function() {
        $scope.myFriends = response.data;
        console.log($scope.myFriends);
      });

    });
  };
}
```

As you can see, the `$scope.loadFriends` function loads the `FB.api` method, making a request to the `me/friends` end point.

The response from the request is stored in the `$scope.myFriends` scope object. Note that we have to manually wrap it within the `$apply` function, because the `FB.api` call is external to the angular-context.

We'll now need to call the `$scope.loadFriends` function after Facebook has been loaded and initialized. So, let's modify the `getLoginStatus` function by adding the following highlighted code:

```
FB.getLoginStatus(function(response) {
  if (response.status == 'connected') {

    FB.api('/me', function(response) {
```

```
      scope.$apply(function() {
        scope.username = response.name;
      })
      console.log(scope.username);
      scope.loadFriends();
    });

  } else {
    FB.login();


  }


})
```

To test and see if the data shows up, let's put in the necessary code in our view.

Add the following code to the `app/partials/partial1.html` file:

```
<div my-facebook></div>
<h1> My Friend's Birthday Reminder</h1>
<div ng-repeat="friend in myFriends">
  {{friend.name}}
</div>
```

We use an `ng-repeat` directive to display our friends' names.

Save the file and refresh the browser to see the changes to take effect. After a few seconds, you should be able to see your list of friends being displayed.

 Keep your console open to see the logs and errors, if any.

Getting your friends' profile pictures and birthdays

As of now, we are only displaying the names of our friends; we now need to display their profile picture and their birthdays (if they have updated it on their Facebook profile) too.

By using the Graph Explorer, you'll see that the endpoint that we need to call to get the required information is `/me/friends?fields=birthday,name,picture`.

Let's update the endpoint in our directive controller function by adding the following highlighted code. We make this change in the `app/directives.js` file, shown as follows:

```
$scope.loadFriends = function() {

  FB.api('/me/friends?fields=birthday,name,picture',
function(response) {
    $scope.$apply(function() {
      $scope.myFriends = response.data;
    });

  });
}
```

We'll also need to update our view to create the placeholders for these additional pieces of information. So, let's modify our `app/partials/partial1.html` file as follows:

```
<div my-facebook></div>
<h1>My Friend's Birthdays</h1>

    <table>
        <thead>
            <tr>
                <th>#</th>
                <th>Friend</th>
                <th>Birthday</th>
            </tr>
        </thead>
        <tbody>
            <tr ng-repeat="friend in myFriends">
                <td>{{$index+1}}</td>
                <td>
                    <img ng-src="{{friend.picture.data.url}}">{
                    {friend.name}}</td>
                <td>{{friend.birthday}}</td>
            </tr>

        </tbody>

    </table>
```

 We use the ng-src directive instead of the regular src to ensure that the browser waits for the AngularJS expression to resolve before it makes the request for the image.

You'll notice that we are now using a `<table>` tag to display the list of friends. In the first column, that is, the serial number, we use the expression `{{$index+1}}` because the value for `$index` starts with `0` while we'd like our count to start from `1`.

Next, we want to display the profile picture in the `<image>` tag, the JSON path for which is `friend.picture.data.url`. This is followed by the profile name and birthday.

Save the file and refresh the page in the browser to see the updated information.

You'll notice that while the profile picture and name is displayed correctly, the birthdays are not showing up. This is because displaying a friend's birthday requires additional permissions. By default, `FB.login` will authenticate with basic permissions only.

As we are going to need additional permissions to display a friend's birthday, let's see how to make a request for these additional permissions.

Requesting additional permission with FB.login

As already mentioned earlier, the `FB.login()` function will authenticate the user with basic level permissions. Any additional permissions that are required need to be passed as comma-separated values to the login function, which is shown as follows:

```
FB.login(function(response) {
}, {scope: 'email,user_likes'});
```

While we can simply update the login function in our directive to pass the `friends_birthday` parameter, it would no longer remain extendable. Ideally, we would like it such that at the time of placing the directive in our view, we should pass on these permissions as additional attributes to our directive. This is done by making use of the `scope` option.

The `scope` option in a directive is used to declare and accept values that are passed to the directive as attributes. In our case, we'll create a `scope` variable named `permissions`, as highlighted in our `app/directives.js` file:

```
scope.username = "John Doe"
},
scope: {
  permissions: '@'
},
controller: function($scope) {
```

An obvious question is: what's the @ symbol doing there? The @ symbol is used to accept a string value from the attribute. The other options are as follows:

- =: This is used to accept an object value and set up a two-way data binding
- &: This is used to accept a function and it will set up a one-way data binding

In our case, since we are passing a string, we use the @ symbol.

Now, the `permissions` variable needs to be called within the `FB.login` function. So, let's do that using the following code snippet:

```
if (response.status == 'connected') {
  FB.api('/me', function(response) {

    scope.$apply(function() {
      scope.username = response.name;
    })
    console.log(scope.username);
    scope.loadFriends();

  });

} else {
FB.login(function(response) {

  }, {
    scope: scope.permissions
  });
}
```

Now, we need to pass the permissions as an attribute to the directive; we will do this in the `app/views/partial1.html` file as follows:

```
<div my-facebook permissions="friends_birthday"></div>
```

To test this, you'll need to log out of Facebook and then refresh our application page.

On refreshing, you should get a popup that asks you to log in and then asks you to allow permissions to share friends' birthdays.

After accepting, you would expect to see your friends along with their birthdays, but strangely, the friends list is blank. The answer to that lies in understanding **isolated scopes**.

Understanding isolated scope

The moment we use the `scope` option of the directive, AngularJS will create an isolated scope for that directive, and all `scope` objects defined within the directive become a part of this isolated scope. In our example, `$scope.myFriends` now becomes a part of the isolated scope.

If you refresh the app in the browser, you will notice that our friends list no longer loads. To be able to pass the `myFriends` object between the directive and its parent controller, we will set up a two-way data binding.

Modify the scope option in the `app/js/directives.js` file by adding the following highlighted code:

```
scope: {
    permissions: '@',
    myFriends: '=friends'
},
```

Next, we will modify our partial to include the `friends` parameter. We will do so by updating the `app/partials/partial1.html` file by adding the following highlighted line:

```
<div my-facebook permissions="friends_birthday" friends='myFriends'></
div>
```

We now have a two-way data binding on the `myFriends` scope and this is now available within the controller. This should now load our friends' data on refreshing the page.

Adding some CSS styles

Now would be a good time to focus on some design and styling for our application. We'll use Bootstrap and a ready-to-use theme from **BootSwatch** to style our application quickly. For this example, we'll use the **SpaceLab** theme. Let's load this theme from `www.bootstrapcdn.com`.

Please open the `index.html` file and make the necessary changes as highlighted in the following code:

```
<!doctype html>
<html lang="en" ng-app="myApp">

<head>
```

```
    <meta charset="utf-8">
    <title>Friend's Birthday Reminder</title>

    <link rel="stylesheet" href="//netdna.bootstrapcdn.com/
bootswatch/3.0.3/spacelab/bootstrap.min.css" />
    <link rel="stylesheet" href="css/app.css" />
  </head>

<body>
    <div class="container">
        <div id="fb-root"></div>
        <div ng-view></div>

    </div>
    <script src="lib/angular/angular.js"></script>
    <script src="lib/angular/angular-route.js"></script>
    <script src="js/app.js"></script>
    <script src="js/services.js"></script>
    <script src="js/controllers.js"></script>
    <script src="js/filters.js"></script>
    <script src="js/directives.js"></script>
  </body>

</html>
```

From the highlighted items in the code, we see that we are loading the CSS for our SpaceLab theme from bootstrapcdn.com.

We are adding the wrapper `<div>` element with a class named container to get our content positioned to the center of the page. We will also get rid of the navigation links and footer text that came with the default AngularJS seed.

Next, let's style the friends listing view in the partial. We'll add the following highlighted CSS classes to the `<table>` tag in the app/views/partial1.html file:

```
<table class="table table-striped">
```

We will also get the welcome message to align right by modifying the code as follows:

```
<div class="text-right" my_facebook permissions=
  "friends_birthday"> </div>
```

Changing the routes

Since we need just one page for now, let's also modify the routes in the `app/app.js` file as follows:

```
'use strict';
// Declare app level module which depends on filters, and services
angular.module('myApp', [
  'ngRoute',
  'myApp.filters',
  'myApp.services',
  'myApp.directives',
  'myApp.controllers'
]).
config(['$routeProvider', function($routeProvider) {
  $routeProvider.when('/', {templateUrl: 'partials/partial1.html',
controller: 'MyCtrl1'});
  $routeProvider.otherwise({redirectTo: '/'});
}]);
```

This will ensure that our page loads directly at `http://localhost:8000/app/index.html#/`. Load this URL in the browser, and it should now display the friends list in a neat-looking tabular format.

However, there is one small problem. The list doesn't quite tell us easily about the upcoming birthdays. We'll need to figure out some logic to sort this list, such that the upcoming birthdays show up first.

Obviously, this is not as easy as simply sorting it by date. You'll also need to take into account that many people haven't added in their birthdays or have only a day and month, while some others have day, month, and year entered for their birthdays. We will need to write a piece of code that takes care of all these scenarios.

We will modify the `$apply` function within the `loadFriends` function in the `app/directives.js` file by using the highlighted code:

```
$scope.$apply(function() {
    var birthdayDate, day;
    var currentYear = new Date().getFullYear();
    var today = new Date().valueOf();
    response.data.forEach(function(data) {
        if (data.birthday) {
            day = data.birthday.split("/");
            birthdayDate = new Date(currentYear, day[0] - 1, day[1]);
            if (birthdayDate.valueOf() < today) {
                birthdayDate.setFullYear(currentYear + 1);
```

```
        }
        data.fromToday = birthdayDate.valueOf() - today;
        data.birthdayDate = birthdayDate;
    }
});
$scope.myFriends = response.data;
console.log($scope.myFriends);
});
```

What we are doing here is splitting the birthday into day, month, and year. We then calculate the current day, month, and year. We convert them both into the UNIX time stamp and then subtract the birthday from today's month and day. The difference is pushed into the data object as a new property called fromToday. We also push the birthdayDate value into the data object because we would like to use this later to format the dates.

Now, on the view, we simply need to sort the result based on the fromToday value. We do that in the app/views/partial1.html file by using the highlighted code:

```
        <tbody>
            <tr ng-repeat="friend in myFriends | orderBy:'fromToday'">
            <td>{{$index+1}}</td>
            <td>
                <img src="{{friend.picture.data.url}}"> {{friend.
name}}</td>
                <td>{{friend.birthday}}</td>
            </tr>

        </tbody>
```

We now have the birthdays sorted with the upcoming birthdays showing up on the top, while the ones that have occurred, go to the bottom of the list.

The default format of the birthdays coming in from Facebook doesn't look very consistent, so, we will format it to display the three-letter month and the date.

This is quite easy in AngularJS as long as you have the date in the correct format. To get this to work, we'll need to make a small change in the app/views/partial1.html file by using the following highlighted code:

```
<td>{{friend.birthdayDate | date:'MMM dd'}}</td>
```

Reload the page, and you should be seeing your friends list with neatly-formatted birthdays.

Adding in the logout link

Now that the app is fully functional, let's add some finishing touches and clean up some code.

What we want to do now is, when the user is logged in, along with the welcome message, we want to show a logout link, which allows the user to log out from the application. We would also want to check the user session, and in case the user is not logged in, then show them the login button instead, just in case the login popup didn't automatically load up.

For all of this, we will need to make changes in the directive template, and since the content in the template is going to be long, we will replace the template option of the directive with the templateURL option.

Change the `template` option in `app/directives.js`, that is, from `template:"Welcome {{username}}"` to `templateUrl: 'partials/greeting. html'`.

We now need to create a new HTML file in the partials folder named `greeting.html`, and add in the following code:

```
<span class="pull-right">
    <span id="welcome" ng-if="logged">Welcome {{username}} | <a
href="#" onclick="FB.logout()">Logout</a>
    </span>
    <span ng-if="!logged">
        <button class="btn btn-primary" ng-click="myLogin()">Login</
button>
    </span>
</span>
```

 Notice that we are using `onclick` for the `FB.logout()` function but `ng-click` for the `myLogin()` function, this is because `onclick` is executed within the context of the window, while `ng-click` is executed within the AngularJS context.

We are using the `ng-if` directive to check if a model named `logged` is `true`, and if so, then display the welcome message and a hyperlink for logout, which when clicked on, calls the `FB.logout()` function.

In case `logged` is `false`, it will display the **Login** button that will call a `scope` function named `myLogin()` which we are going to create shortly.

We will now go into our directive and define the logged `scope` model and the `myLogin` function in the `app/directives.js` file using the highlighted code:

```
FB.getLoginStatus(function(response) {

    if (response.status == 'connected') {
        scope.logged = true;
```

Then, in our directive controller, we'll create our `myLogin()` function, which acts as a wrapper to our `FB.login` function along with the additional permissions request as follows:

```
$scope.myLogin = function() {
  FB.login(function(response) {

  }, {
    scope: $scope.permissions
  });

}
```

With this, our application is all cleaned up and polished. Save your files and refresh the page in the browser to ensure everything is working.

Writing automated tests

Our application is working fine, which is great; however, going forward, you would probably tinker with the code, refactor it, add some additional features, and so on. While doing so, it's important to make sure that we don't break anything.

Moreover, because our app makes use of a third-party API, which at times may go down or change, this will cause our app to fail.

In order to detect any breakages, it is vital that we have some kind of automated tests that can be run periodically or every time something changes in our code.

We will use Karma to run our Unit tests and Protractor for our **End-to-End Testing**.

Writing Unit tests with Karma

Karma is a test runner to run JavaScript Unit tests. We can use Jasmine, Mocha, or QUnit to write our test cases and run it using Karma.

Since we are going to be writing our Unit tests, to test our directive, we will write them in the `test/unit/directivesSpec.js` file.

We will replace the existing contents of this file with the following code:

```
'use strict';

/* jasmine specs for directives go here */

describe('directives', function() {

    var $compile, $rootScope;
    beforeEach(function() {
        module('myApp.directives');
    })
})
```

We will first describe our test case and define our two variables. We then need to load the directives module before running each test case. Hence, we call it within the `beforeEach()` function.

Next, we will inject the `$rootScope` and `$compile` functions as dependencies with the following piece of code:

```
beforeEach(inject(function(_$compile_, _$rootScope_) {
    $compile = _$compile_;
    $rootScope = _$rootScope_;

}));
```

Note that this function is written within the parent `describe` block.

Next, we will write our test case as follows to see if our directive loads and renders correctly:

```
it('should check if directive is loaded', function() {
    var element = $compile("<div my-facebook permission=
        'friends_birthday'> </div>")($rootScope);
    $rootScope.$digest();
    expect(element.text()).toContain("Login");
})
```

As you can see from the preceding code, we first render our directive using the `$compile` function and then test to see if the output of the compiled directive contains the word "Login".

To run our tests, we can simply run the following command in the terminal:

```
npm test
```

Once you run this script, you'll notice a Chrome window being initialized, and you'll see the output of the various actions being logged in the terminal.

You'll also notice our test case failing with an error output saying something like the following:

```
Error: Unexpected request: GET partials/greeting.html
No more request expected at $httpBackend (/test/lib/angular/angular-mocks.js:1177:9)
```

The reason our test failed is because while running unit tests, all HTTP calls to external resources are mocked. In this case, our directive makes a call to an external file named greeting.html, and since that request isn't executed, our directive template code doesn't load, and hence the test case fails.

Had we used the template option instead of templateUrl, our test case would have passed because there was no need for that external call.

The work around for this problem is by prefilling $templateCache with the contents of our directive template. As a rule, AngularJS will first check for contents in $templateCache and will request the external resource only when it is not available in $templateCache.

We will modify our injector function to prefill $templateCache by using the following highlighted code:

```
beforeEach(inject(function(_$compile_, _$rootScope_, $templateCache) {
        $compile = _$compile_;
        $rootScope = _$rootScope_;
$templateCache.put('partials/greeting.html', '<span
class="pull-right"><span id="welcome" ng-if="logged">Welcome
{{username}} | <a href="#" onclick="FB.logout()">Logout</a></
span><span ng-if="!logged"><button class="btn btn-primary" ng-
click="myLogin()">Login</button></span></span>
')

    }));
```

Save the file and notice Karma automatically rerun your tests in the console; this time, your test case should pass.

Another approach to prefilling $templateCache is by using the **html2js** preprocessor, where the contents of the HTML are stored as html.js files. This is more suitable when you don't want to manually push the directive template contents into $templateCache.

Writing End-to-End tests using Protractor

Protractor is now the default tool for End-to-End testing in AngularJS. Protractor makes use of Selenium and WebdriverJS to run its test.

> To know how to install the Selenium standalone server, refer to the *Installing Selenium Standalone Server* section in *Chapter 2, Setting Up Your Rig* of this book.

Now, let's open our test/protractor-conf.js file and change the value of browserName from chrome to firefox.

Next, we'll write our End-to-End test in the test/e2e/scenarios.js file as follows:

```
describe('Enter Facebook credentials', function() {
    var ptor = protractor.getInstance();
    it('should log in & put User and Pass', function() {
        browser.get('http://localhost:8000/app/index.html');

    })
})
```

First, we create the instances of the protractor object and then we define our test case. The browser.get() line will launch Firefox and navigate to the mentioned URL.

Next, we'll continue writing the following code within the it() function:

```
var currentWindowHandle = ptor.getWindowHandle();
var angularElement = element(by.className('btn-primary'));
angularElement.click();
ptor.sleep(5000);
var handlesPromise = ptor.getAllWindowHandles();
```

What we are doing here is, we first get the window handle of the current window and store it in a variable. Then, we navigate and click on the **Login** button. We identify it by the class name associated with it. This will launch a popup. Next, we get all the available window handles and store them in an array.

Continuing further, we add the rest of the code as follows:

```
handlesPromise
    .then(function(handles) {

        return ptor.switchTo().window(handles[1]);
    }).then(function(handle) {

        browser.driver.findElement(by.id("email")).sendKeys("name@
email.com");
        browser.driver.findElement(by.id("pass")).
sendKeys("myPassword");
        browser.driver.findElement(by.name("login")).click();
        ptor.switchTo().window(currentWindowHandle);

    ptor.sleep(2000)
    browser.refresh();
    ptor.sleep(2000)
        var msg = element(by.id('welcome')).getText();

        expect(msg).toContain("Welcome < YOUR NAME >");

})
```

Next, using the promise, we switch the focus to the popup window, and then we fill in the e-mail and password fields, and click on the **Login** button.

Once the **Login** button is clicked on, we switch the focus back to our main page.

We then wait for a few seconds and refresh the page to give our app some time to populate the data from Facebook. We then check to see if the welcome message matches the one we have defined.

Save the file and test using the following terminal command:

```
protractor test/protractor-conf.js
```

Watch the script launch the browser and fill the details in the popup. After the test is complete, the browser will close automatically, and in the terminal, you should be able to see the following message:

1 test, 1 assertion, 0 failures

This completes our first End-to-End test. Go ahead and write a couple more tests.

Summary

Congratulations! We accomplished quite a few things in this chapter!

We learned about the Facebook Social Graph and the Graph APIs. We saw how to use the Graph Explorer tool, which is a really good tool for better understanding the various features of the Graph API.

We saw how Facebook login works and how to request additional permissions when you need to access data that is beyond the default dataset.

We saw what directives were and why they are so useful in integrating external plugins into our AngularJS application. We saw the various options in the directive and how they function.

Last but not least, we got a brief understanding of how AngularJS updates the data from the model in the views using `$watch` during the `$digest` loops and how `$apply` is used to trigger a `$digest` loop.

In the next chapter, we'll see how to build a responsive mobile application by making use of some nifty HTML5 features.

6
Building an Expense Manager Mobile App

Hello folks! Hope you are enjoying your journey so far.

In the previous chapter, we learned about directives, one of the most important features of AngularJS. We saw how to leverage directives to wrap third-party plugins and authentication modules.

We saw how to build a Facebook friend's Birthday Reminder app, and while doing so, we learned about the Facebook SDK, FB authentication, and how to use the Graph Explorer.

In this chapter, we will go about building a simple **Expense Manager App** optimized for mobile and tablet devices.

Some of the interesting things that we'll learn are as follows:

- Understanding HTML5 **Web Storage**
- Making the app responsive in order to fit different screen resolutions
- Integrating **Data-Driven Documents** (**D3**) Graph APIs to generate graphs
- Optimizing the app for touch and gesture inputs
- Converting the app into a web app

This chapter is going to be relatively design-focused, so make sure you have your creative juices flowing freely and your CSS skills all sharpened up.

Understanding HTML5 Web Storage

Web Storage is an HTML5 feature that allows you to store data on the client side. Web Storage consists of two objects, `localStorage` and `sessionStorage`.

localStorage

The `localStorage` object is a single persistent object, which is stored on the local device. It is available even when the browser window is closed and the cache and cookies are cleared.

Saving data in `localStorage` is as easy as writing; one can do so in either of the following ways:

- `window.localStorage['name']= 'John Doe';`
- `window.localStorage.setItem('name','John Doe');`

In the preceding code, `name` is the key, and `John Doe` is the value that we are associating with the key.

Reading data from `localStorage` is equally easy; one can do so in either of the following ways:

- `var myName = localStorage['name']`
- `var myName = localStorage.getItem('name')`

A couple of things to remember about `localStorage` are as follows:

- The data in `localStorage` is always stored as strings in simple key value pairs

- The `localStorage` object is sandboxed and tied to a single origin, that is, accessing and modifying data in `localStorage` can happen only from the domain it was created from

- The `localStorage` object is unique to each browser/client, and each browser allocates a maximum of 5 MB of space for `localStorage` for each domain

- Saving and retrieval of data from `localStorage` happens in a synchronous mode, which means, further processing of the script is halted until its execution is complete

- The `localStorage` object is supported across all browsers and also supported in iOS and Android

- Performance bottlenecks can arise when we are using `localStorage` to save and retrieve large amounts of data

sessionStorage

The sessionStorage object functions just like localStorage, with the only exception that the data is lost once the browser window is closed.

Building the Expense Manager App

Now that we have a better understanding of Web Storage, let's use it to build our Expense Manager Application.

Like in the previous chapters, we will use the forked angular-seed project, which is available at https://github.com/areai51/angular-seed.

Let's create a folder named exp-mgr, and extract the contents of the angular-seed ZIP file into the folder.

Run the following command in the terminal to install the dependencies:

```
npm install
```

Let's start by tweaking the base index file located at app/index.html. We will replace the default HTML markup with the following code:

```html
<!doctype html>
<html lang="en" ng-app="myApp">
<head>
    <meta charset="utf-8">
<meta name="viewport" content="width=device-width, user-scalable=no">
    <title>Expense Manager</title>
    <link rel="stylesheet" href="css/app.css" />
</head>
<body>
    <h1>Expense Manager</h1>

    <div class="container">
        <div class="page-slide" ng-view></div>
    </div>
    <script src="bower_components/angular/angular.js"></script>
    <script src="bower_components/angular-route/angular-route.js"></script>
    <script src="js/app.js"></script>
    <script src="js/services.js"></script>
    <script src="js/controllers.js"></script>
    <script src="js/filters.js"></script>
```

```
    <script src="js/directives.js"></script>
</body>

</html>
```

Most of this is standard HTML markup and shouldn't need much explanation. An important line to note is the following:

```
<meta name="viewport" content="width=device-width,
  user-scalable=no">
```

The preceding line of code is necessary so that the page doesn't scale when viewed on mobile devices.

As we would like meaningful URL links, we will update them along with our routes, so please make the following necessary changes in the app/js/app.js file:

```
config(['$routeProvider',
  function($routeProvider) {
    $routeProvider.when('/', {
      templateUrl: 'partials/home.html',
      controller: 'HomeCtrl'
    });
    $routeProvider.when('/add-expense', {
      templateUrl: 'partials/add-expense.html',
      controller: 'AddExpenseCtrl'
    });
    $routeProvider.when('/view-summary', {
      templateUrl: 'partials/view-summary.html',
      controller: 'ViewSummaryCtrl'
    });
    $routeProvider.otherwise({
      redirectTo: '/'
    });
  }
]);
```

Here, we are defining our routes and mapping them to the respective controllers and partials.

 Don't forget to rename your partial files to match `templateUrl`, as defined in the preceding code.

We will also need to create a new partial file named `partials/home.html` with the following content:

```
<ul class="menu">
    <li><a href="#/add-expense">Add Expense</a>
    </li>
    <li><a href="#/view-summary">View Summary</a>
    </li>
</ul>
```

We will also need to create an `empty HomeCtrl` function in our `app/js/controllers.js` file as follows:

```
.controller('HomeCtrl',function(){
})
```

Let's quickly test to see if the links are working.

To start your node server, navigate to the `exp-mgt` folder, and type in the following command in the terminal.

npm start

In your browser, navigate to the following URL to make sure that everything is working:

`http://localhost:8000/app/index.html#/`

As you will already know, mobile apps need to look elegant and classy. Following the trends of a flat user interface, let's style our app.

We are going to make use of Google web fonts to apply a consistent thin font for the entire app.

For this exercise, we will choose a font called **Lato**, which is available at the following link:

`http://www.google.com/fonts/specimen/Lato`

To include this font into our application, we'll include the following stylesheet, as highlighted, in our `app/index.html` file:

```
<title>Expense Manager</title>
    <link href='http://fonts.googleapis.com/css?family=Lato:100'
        rel='stylesheet' type='text/css'>
    <link rel="stylesheet" href="css/app.css" />
```

Next, we would like to have a background image that would randomly change each time you start the application.

So, let's add an `<image>` tag as follows:

```
<h1>Expense Manager</h1>
    <img class="bg-image" src="http://lorempixel.com/
        1024/768/business/">
    <div class="container">
```

We'll make use of `www.lorempixel.com`, a great site to generate stock images.

Now, it's time to add the following necessary CSS styles in our `app/css/app.css` file; make sure that you delete all the boilerplate CSS styles that were initially present:

```css
body {
    font-family:'Lato', sans-serif;
    font-weight: 100;
    color:#f9f9f9;
    background: #333;
    height: 100%;

}
.bg-image {
    position: fixed;
    top: 0;
    left:0;
    min-width: 100%;
    min-height: 100%;
    z-index: -1;
    background: #333;
    opacity: 0.3;
}
h1 {
    font-size: 2.5em;
    font-weight: 100;
    margin-left: 5%;

}
```

In the preceding code, we are setting Lato with a font weight of `100` as the default font for all text in the app. We set the background color to dark gray, and the text color to an off-white color.

The `bg-image` class is used to set the background image to `100%` of the screen size and also give it a slight transparency so that the text is readable over the image. Note that we set the `z-index` parameter to a negative value to make sure that the image loads under the text.

Now, let's style the menu. We will style our app more or less on the lines of a Windows 8 phone app as follows:

```
.menu {
  list-style: none;
  margin-bottom: 2em;
  padding: 0 0 0.5em;
  position: absolute;
  bottom: 1em;
}
.menu li {
  margin: 2em 1em;
}
.menu a {
  color: #f9f9f9;
  font-size: 2em;
  text-decoration: none
}
```

The preceding code simply sets the font size and color of the navigation links. It also sets the links aligned from the bottom.

Note that we are using em instead of px as the unit of measurement to define the sizes, widths, and so on. This is important, because we want the sizes to be in proportion to the device it is viewed on.

We should now have our basic look and feel in place. Hope your app looks something like the following screenshot:

Building the Add Expense form

Now, let's create our Add Expense form. We will add the following code in the `app/partials/add-expense.html` file:

```
<h2>Add Expense</h2>
<form id="addForm" name="addForm" novalidate >
    <label>Category</label>
    <select ng-model="expense.category"
        ng-options="category for category in categories">
    </select>
    <label>Amount:</label>
    <input type="number" ng-model="expense.amount"></input>
    <label>Description:</label>
    <input type="text" ng-model="expense.description"></input>
    <button ng-click="submit()">Submit</button>
</form>
```

This is a rather straightforward form. The `novalidate` tag in HTML5 is used to disable the browser's default validations.

Notice that we are also making use of the built-in directive, `ng-options`, to dynamically load the category list into our select box.

We'll style the form by adding the following CSS to the `app/css/app.css` file:

```
.page-slide input , .page-slide select{
  display: block;
  padding:0.75em;
  margin: .5em 0 1em 0;
width: 90%;
font-size:1em;
border: thin solid #ccc;
}

button{
  background: #3E7504 ;
  color:#CCFF96;
  border: thin solid #3E7504;
  padding: 3px 8px;
  font-size: 1.2em;
}
```

Now, let's make the form functional.

As you can see, the first item on the form is a select box, which is supposed to show the list of categories. We could easily create a scope model within the controller and define the list of items as an array. However, we are going to need the same list of categories on our **View Summary** page too; hence, we will need to figure out a way to have it defined at one place but be available in both controllers. There are a couple of ways we could share the data between the two controllers. One is by making use of $rootScope and the other is using a service.

What is $rootScope?

Every AngularJS application has a single root scope. The scope within every controller would inherit the properties of $rootScope. Thus, any model defined in $rootScope is available on all controller scopes.

We can access the root scope using the $rootScope key.

We can compare $rootScope to the global variables in JavaScript. Properties and methods defined in $rootScope are accessible all throughout the application.

Understanding the .run block

Now that we know what $rootScope is, the next question that arises is how do we set the $rootScope variables at the time of loading the application.

A $rootScope variable can be set from within any controller or directive. However, if you want to set the variables at the time of initialization of the app, then we need to make use of the .run block.

A .run block is similar to a .config block, which we've used in the past to define our routes in $routeProvider.

The .run block is used to initialize the application.

> One must be careful with putting too many things within $rootScope, because variables and objects defined within $rootScope are not available for Garbage collection throughout the life of the application.

The other and more appropriate way of sharing data between controllers is to make use of a Service. As we have already learned in *Chapter 4, Using REST Web Services in Your AngularJS App*, that services are singletons and persist throughout the life of the app, we can leverage them to share data between the controllers.

Creating a value service to store CategoryList

As we want our category list available within different controllers in our application, we will create it as a value service.

Let's open our `app/js/services.js` file and add the following code:

```
.value('categoryList', ["Food", "Fuel", "Grocery",
  "Entertainment"])
```

We'll also need to inject `categoryList` into our `AddExpenseCtrl` controller located in the `app/js/controllers.js` file as follows:

```
.controller('AddExpenseCtrl', ['$scope', 'categoryList',
    function($scope, categoryList) {
        $scope.categories = categoryList;
    }
]);
```

Navigate to your `add-expense` page in the browser at `http://localhost:8000/app/index.html#/add-expense`, and make sure that the category dropdown is now showing the options we defined in `categoryList`.

Validating the Add Expense form

Client-side form validations in AngularJS are extremely easy. AngularJS takes advantage of HTML5's built-in form validations and builds on top of it.

We can set validations for a field by simply setting it as a required field or setting its data type to `text`, `number`, or `email`.

The following table shows the various options we can use for form validations:

Validation Option	Description
`<input type="text" required />`	This sets the field as a required field
`<input type="text" ng-minlength=7 />`	This sets the minimum length of the input box to 7
`<input type="text" ng-maxlength=15 />`	This sets the maximum length of the input box to 15
`<input type="number"/>`	This validates for numeric input
`<input type="url" />`	This validates for URL input
`<input type="email" name="email" />`	This validates for a valid e-mail address
`<input type="text" ng-pattern="/[a-zA-Z0-9]/ " />`	The `ng-pattern` directive allows us to put in regular expressions

Based on these validation rules, Angular JS will apply certain CSS classes to these form elements. The classes it applies are as follows:

CSS class name	Description
`.ng-pristine {}`	This class is applied at the time the form is loaded. This is to allow overriding the properties in the `ng-invalid` class when the form is blank.
`.ng-dirty {}`	This class is applied when the form data has been modified.
`.ng-valid {}`	This class is applied when the field matches the validation rules.
`.ng-invalid {}`	This class is applied when the field doesn't match the validation rules.

Let's add validations to our `add-expenses` form. Update the `app/partials/add-expense.html` file, as highlighted in the following code:

```
<h2>Add Expense</h2>
<form id="addForm" name="addForm" novalidate>
    <label>Category:</label>
    <select ng-model="expense.category"
        ng-options="category for category in categories">
    <label>Amount:</label>
    <input required type="number"
        ng-model="expense.amount"></input>
    <label>Description:</label>
    <input type="text" ng-pattern="/^[a-zA-Z 0-9]*$/"
        ng-model="expense.description"></input>
    <button ng-disabled="addForm.$pristine || addForm.$dirty &&
        addForm.$invalid" ng-click="submit()">Submit</button>
</form>
```

We set the `Amount` textbox to `required` and the data type to `number`. We also set the `Description` textbox to accept only alphanumeric characters and not accept any special characters.

We also make use of the `ng-disabled` directive to disable our **Submit** button until all the form fields are valid.

Next, we'll add the validation CSS classes with styling properties to highlight invalid fields with a red background and valid fields with a green background.

We'll add the following classes to our `app/css/app.css` file:

```css
#addForm .ng-pristine {
    background: none!important;
}
#addForm .ng-dirty {
    background:#FAC8C8;
}
#addForm .ng-valid {
    background: #E8FAC8
}
#addForm .ng-invalid {
    background: #FAC8C8
}
button:disabled {
    background: #ccc;
    color:#aaa;
}
```

Notice that we are using `!important` to force `.ng-pristine` to override the `.ng-invalid` class when the form is just loaded.

Save the file, refresh the `add-expense.html` file in the browser, and check out the form validations in action. Notice how the background color changes as you type into the form fields. Also notice the **Submit** button turning from gray to green once all the fields are valid.

Using localStorage to save data

At the start of this chapter, under the *Understanding HTML5 Web Storage* section, we saw what `localStorage` is and how to use it. We will now make use of it to store the expenses added using the `add-expense` form.

AngularJS best practices recommend that we make use of a factory to store or retrieve data from external sources.

Let's create our factory that will save the form data into `localStorage`:

We'll add our code to the `app/js/services.js` file as follows:

```javascript
.factory('expService', [function() {
  var prefix = 'exp-mgr';
  return {
    saveExpense: function(data) {
      var timeStamp = Math.round(new Date().getTime());
      var key = prefix + timeStamp;
```

```
            data = JSON.stringify(data);
            localStorage[key] = data;
        }
    };
}]);
```

Ideally, just the following line of code is all that is needed to store our data in
localStorage:

```
localStorage[key] = data;
```

Let's see why the rest of the code is equally important.

Firstly, we are creating a prefix for all data that is being stored as a part of this app.
Remember that localStorage stores data as simple key-value pairs. These keys are
unique to each domain. To make sure that we are interacting with data belonging to
only our app and to also to make it easier while retrieving the data, we prefix all our
keys with the exp-mgr prefix.

Next, in our return function, we create a function named saveExpense; this will be
called when the **Submit** button of the form is hit. The saveExpense function takes in
the data as an input parameter.

Next, we use the timestamp to generate our unique key and add the prefix to it. As
localStorage can store the values only as strings, we need to convert our JSON
data into a string. This is exactly what we do in our next step using the JSON.
stringify() method.

Finally, we store the converted string into localStorage as the value to our
timestamped key.

We now need to write our submit function within the controller in the app/js/
controllers.js file, as highlighted in the following code:

```
.controller('AddExpenseCtrl', ['$scope', 'categoryList','expService',f
unction($scope, categoryList,expService) {
        $scope.categories = categoryList;
        $scope.submit = function() {

    expService.saveExpense($scope.expense);
    };
    }
]);
```

Notice that we are injecting our expService factory into the controller along with $scope.

The $scope.submit function simply calls the saveExpense method of our expService factory and passes the form data, which is stored in the expense model.

Refresh the **Add Expense** page, fill up the form, and hit the **Submit** button. As long as you don't get any errors in your console, we can safely assume that our data has been saved into localStorage. Obviously, this is not convincing enough; we would want to see the data that is being stored.

For this, let's create our next factory function named getExpense.

Let's open up app/js/services.js and add our getExpense function as follows:

```
getExpense: function() {
    var expenses = [];
    var prefixLength = prefix.length;
    Object.keys(localStorage)
        .forEach(function(key) {
            if (key.substring(0, prefixLength) == prefix) {
                var item = window.localStorage[key];
                item = JSON.parse(item);
                expenses.push(item);
            }
        });

    return expenses;
}
```

 Make sure that you have a comma at the end of the earlier saveExpense function.

Another point to note about localStorage is that it doesn't have advanced methods to filter data or return a set of matching records. We need to iterate through each item in localStorage and selectively pick up the ones that match our needs.

This is what we are doing in our getExpense function.

We first get the length of our prefix. Then, using forEach, we iterate through each item present in localStorage, match it to our prefix key, and push the matching entries into an array called expenses.

Notice that we are using JSON.parse to convert our stringified data back into JSON format.

We now need to write our controller to receive this data. As we want to display the result on the **View Summary** page, we'll write our code in the ViewSummaryCtrl function.

Let's create our ViewSummaryCtrl with the following highlighted code in the app/js/controllers.js file.

```
.controller('ViewSummaryCtrl', ['$scope',
'expService',function($scope, expService) {
        $scope.expenses = expService.getExpense();


    }
]);
```

To be able to view this data, let's add the necessary code in our view partial located at app/partials/view-summary.html:

```
<h2>Expense Details</h2>
<div class="exp-details" ng-repeat="expense in expenses">
  <div class="col-sm-1">{{$index+1}} </div>
  <div class="col-sm-3">{{expense.category}} </div>
  <div class="col-sm-4"> {{expense.description}}</div>
  <div class="col-sm-2">{{expense.amount| currency:"$"}} </div>

</div>
```

Navigate to the **View Summary** page in the browser, and you should be able to see some data under **Expense Details**. This data is obviously unformatted and unreadable.

Notice that we are adding the currency filter to display the amount. This would automatically format the amount to prefix the $ sign and add 2 decimal places to the amount.

Let's add some CSS styles to make it a bit more readable.

Add the following CSS classes to the app/css/app.css file:

```
.exp-details {
  clear: both;
}
.exp-details >div {
  float: left;
  padding: 0.5em 0.2em;
```

```
    border-bottom: thin solid #eaeaea;
}
.exp-details .col-sm-1 {
  width:5%;
}
.exp-details .col-sm-2 {
  width:20%;
}
.exp-details .col-sm-3 {
  width:25%;
}.exp-details .col-sm-4 {
  width:40%;
}
```

The preceding sets of classes position the `<div>` elements next to each other and assign varying widths.

Notice that we are using Bootstrap3-style class names here.

The reason we are rewriting our own classes and not simply including Bootstrap is because we want to keep our application's footprints as small as possible. As we are going to be using less than 20 percent of the classes defined in Bootstrap, it's better to simply rewrite them.

Save the file, refresh the page, and make sure your Details table is looking a lot cleaner now. Go ahead and add in a couple of dummy expenses to see how it shows up on the **Details** page.

Building a bar chart directive based on D3

Besides simply showing a list of all the expenses entered, it would be a lot meaningful if we can also display a summary of the total expenses across the categories as a bar chart.

We will build our own custom bar chart directive that will generate graphs based on the inputs provided.

For this, we will use the D3 JavaScript library to create a SVG-based bar graph.

 Complete details on D3 and various examples of how to use it are available at `http://d3js.org/`.

An important thing to remember about the D3 library is that D3 is not a ready-to-use graphing library, where you pass the data values and define what type of graph you want.

D3 could be thought of as jQuery, but for data visualization. D3 simply provides a set of APIs to easily update and manage the DOM.

So, while bar graphs are amongst the most basic type of graphs, D3 can be used to build fairly complex and highly interactive data visualizations.

Summarizing the expenses by categories

Getting back to our application, as we want to create a graph showing the summary of expenses for each category, we will first need to calculate the total expense made under each category.

We will start by creating a function within our factory service that will total up the expenses for a category name that is passed to it.

Open up the app/js/services.js file, and add the following function within the return {} section of the expService factory:

```
getCategoryTotal: function(category) {
  var categoryTotal = 0;
  var prefixLength = prefix.length;
  Object.keys(localStorage)
    .forEach(function(key) {
      if (key.substring(0, prefixLength) == prefix) {
        var item = localStorage[key]
        item = JSON.parse(item)
        if (item.category == category) {
          categoryTotal += parseFloat(item.amount);
        }

      }

    });
  return categoryTotal;
}
```

For the sake of simplicity, we are directly creating our methods within the `return` statement of the factory. You may also choose to define the methods outside of `return` and include a handle to the function in the `return` statement in the following manner:

```
var getCategoryTotal = function(){//code}
return {
  getCategoryTotal: getCategoryTotal
}
```

The preceding function is very similar to our `getExpense` function, where we are iterating through the list of keys in `localStorage` and picking up the data that is matching our app.

Once we get the entries for our app, we then parse it to get back the JSON output.

Once we have the output in the JSON format, we then further iterate and total up the amounts where the category name matches the name passed to the function.

Notice that we need to use `parseFloat` to convert our numbers from string to a float value before we total them up.

Next, in order to get the total for each of the categories in our list, we will write a `forEach` loop in our controller that will give us this data.

Add the following code in the `ViewSummaryCtrl` function located in the `app/js/controllers.js` file:

```
$scope.summaryData = [];

var categories=categoryList categories
    .forEach(function(item) {
        var catTotal = expService.getCategoryTotal(item);

        $scope.summaryData.push({
            category: item,
            amount: catTotal
        });

    });
```

As we are using `categoryList` here, don't forget to add it as a dependency to the `ViewSummaryCtrl` function, as highlighted in the following code:

```
.controller('ViewSummaryCtrl', ['$scope', 'categoryList',
'$expService',
    function($scope, categoryList, $expService) {
```

To verify that everything is working correctly and to view the category totals, we'll add the following temporary piece of code to our `view-summary` partial located in the `app/partials/view-summary.html` file:

```
<h2>Expense Summary</h2>
<div ng-repeat="sum in summaryData">
  <div> {{sum.category}} - {{sum.amount}}</div>

</div>
```

Refresh the **View Summary** page in the browser, and make sure that the category totals are being calculated correctly.

Creating our bar chart directive

Now that we have our category totals in place, let's work on creating our bar chart directive that will display the graph based on these category totals.

Let's start by including the `d3.js` library in the `app/index.html` file, as highlighted in the following code:

```
<script src="http://d3js.org/d3.v3.min.js" charset="utf-8"></script>
```

Now, we will start writing our directive in the `app/js/directives.js` file as follows:

```
.directive('barChart', ['$document', '$window',
  function($document, $window) {
    return {
      scope: {
        data: '=',

      },

      link: function(scope, element, attrs) {

      },

      template: '<div id="chart"></div>'
    }
  }
])
```

As we can see from the preceding code, we are calling our directive `barChart` and injecting the document and window services into it.

In the scope options, we define an object called `data`, which will receive the values to generate the graph. Notice that we are using the = symbol instead of @.

The `link` option, for now, is an empty function, but this is where we will be writing all our code.

The `template` option creates an empty wrapper `<div>` element with an identifier called `chart`. This wrapper `<div>` element will hold our D3 bar chart within it.

Let's call this directive into our view by adding the directive to the `app/partials/view-summary.html` file:

```
<h2>Expense Summary</h2>
<div bar-chart data='summaryData' ></div>
```

As you can see, we are passing `summaryData` as the input to build the graphs.

Next, we create a function called `drawGraph()`, which will be responsible for drawing the graph for us.

```
link: function(scope, element, attrs) {
var chart = d3.select('#chart')
        .append('svg')
        .style('width', '95%');

  scope.drawGraph = function(data) {

  }
scope.drawGraph(scope.data)
}
```

The code so far stores the d3 object instance in the chart variable; it then creates the `svg` tag within the `<div>` element and sets the width of the `svg` tag to 95% of its parent `<div>`. The reason we set it to 95 and not 100 is so that the bars don't touch the right-hand side corners.

Next, we will declare some variables and objects that we'll need within our drawGraph function:

```
var barHeight = 20,
   barGap = 5,
   graphOrigin = 150,
   chartWidth = chart.style('width'),
   chartHeight = scope.data.length * (barHeight + barGap),
   color = d3.scale.category10(),
   xScale = d3.scale.linear()
```

```
    .domain([0, d3.max(data, function(d) {
      return d.amount;
    })])
    .range([0, chartWidth]);
  chart.attr('height', chartHeight);
```

Let's understand what these variables mean. They are described in detail in the following table:

Variable Name	Description
barHeight	The height for each bar of the bar chart.
barGap	The gap between two bars.
graphOption	The starting point from where the graph will be drawn. Look at it as a left margin for the bars.
chartWidth	The width for the entire chart; in this case, it is the width of the chart's element.
chartHeight	The height for the entire chart. This is calculated dynamically depending on the number of items in the data array multiplied by the bar's height.
color	The colors for the bars. D3 comes with the following four color palettes by default: • .category10() will generate a palette for 10 category colors. • .category20() will generate a palette for 20 colors. • .category20b() and .category20c() are two additional palettes with varying colors of the 20-color palette.
xScale	d3.scale.linear() will generate the relevant output range for a given set of inputs. This ensures that the graph will automatically adapt irrespective of whether the input data values are small or very large numbers.
.domain	Takes an array as the input, and sets the starting and ending values of the input data.
.range	Takes an array as the input with the starting and ending values of the output to draw the graph.

After setting the initial values for the variables, let's start with drawing the bars, as follows:

```
chart.selectAll('myBars')
  .data(data)
  .enter()
  .append('rect')
```

```
    .attr('height', barHeight)
    .attr('x', graphOrigin)
    .attr('y', function(d, i) {
        return i * (barHeight + barGap);
    })
    .attr('fill', function(d) {
        return color(d.amount);
    })
    .attr('width', function(d) {
        return xScale(d.amount);
    });
```

As we can see, we first select all the `rect` elements. Then, as per the number of items in the data object, we append a `rect` element after the last element with its height, x and y positions, color, and width.

An interesting thing to note is that `chart.selectAll('myBars')` will return null the first time, but D3 understands this and will automatically add it the first time and continue from there.

Save the file, and refresh the **View Summary** page to see the bars being drawn.

Next, we display the category labels with the following code:

```
chart.selectAll('categoryLabel')
    .data(data)
    .enter()
    .append('text')
    .attr('fill', '#fff')
    .attr('y', function(d, i) {
        return i * (barHeight + barGap) + 10;
    })
    .attr('x', (graphOrigin - 5))
    .attr('text-anchor', 'end')
    .text(function(d) {
        return d.category;
    });
```

From the preceding code, we are now attaching the text element and setting the font color to white. As we want to display the labels to the left of the graph, we set their x attribute to (graphOrigin - 5). However, we also want the text to be aligned to the right. We do this by setting text-anchor to end.

Next, we would also like to display the actual values over the bars; the following piece of code will do this:

```
chart.selectAll('values')
  .data(data)
  .enter()
  .append('text')
  .attr('fill', '#fff')
  .attr('y', function(d, i) {
    return i * (barHeight + barGap) + 15;
  })
  .attr('x', (graphOrigin + 5))
  .attr('text-anchor', 'start')
  .text(function(d) {
    return d.amount;
  });
```

Refresh the page, and watch the bar chart in action.

Your bar chart should look something like the following screenshot:

Making the app responsive

Responsive Web Design (RWD) is a design approach where the layout of an app adjusts automatically to provide the most optimum viewing experience on the device or screen size on which the app is being viewed.

Responsive designs are built by making use of the CSS3 media query feature, where one can apply different CSS properties for an element based on certain conditions that it satisfies.

In our current application, we would like the **View Summary** page to display the graph and expense details side by side when viewed on a large screen. However, when viewed on a mobile, we would like the graph to show up the preceding details table in a single column.

While doing so, we also need to make sure that the graph scales automatically, depending on the screen size.

Adding the CSS media query

As we want to alter the positions of the graph and details table depending on the screen size, let's first wrap each of them within individual divs for easier manipulation.

Please update the `app/partials/view-summary.html` file, which is highlighted as follows:

```html
<div id="summary">
    <h2>Expense Summary</h2>
    <div bar-chart data='summaryData'></div>
</div>
<div id="details">
    <h2>Expense Details</h2>
    <div class="exp-details" ng-repeat="expense in expenses">
        <div class="span1">{{$index+1}}</div>
        <div class="span3">{{expense.category}}</div>
        <div class="span4">{{expense.description}}</div>
        <div class="span2">{{expense.amount|currency:"$" }}</div>

    </div>
</div>
```

Next, let's add the CSS for media query in the `app/css/app.css` file as follows:

```css
@media all and (min-width: 680px){
  #summary,#details{
    float:left;
    width:49%;
    padding: 0.25em;
  }
}
```

The preceding code checks if the screen width is 680 px or greater, and if this condition is true, then it would apply the CSS for the `#summary` and `#details` divs.

The CSS that it applies will float the `<div>` elements to the left and set their width to `49%` of the screen size, along with a padding of `0.25` em.

The reason we set the width of `49%` instead of `50%` is to account for the padding space.

Save the file, and refresh the **View Summary** page.

Drag the browser to see the responsive design in action. The page should switch from the two-column layout to a single-column layout when you reduce the browser window width to less than 680 px.

The mobile view of the app should look like the following screenshot:

For the desktop or horizontal view, the app should look like the following, in a two-column layout:

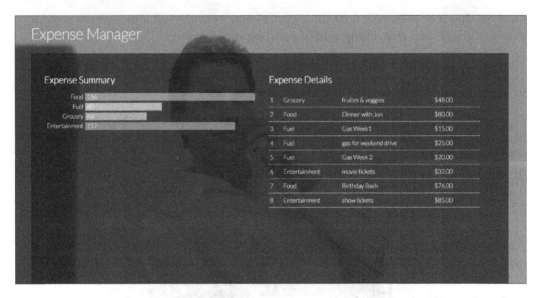

While the responsive design works fine, you'll notice that the bar chart doesn't seem to scale. Instead, it gets cropped as the window is being reduced. Let's fix this.

Scaling the D3 chart based on window size

The reason our bar chart doesn't resize as per the window size is because once the `chartWidth` variable gets initialized with the initial value, there are no triggers or events coded in that will recalculate its value.

Thankfully, we can make use of `$window.onresize` to detect whether the window has been resized and redraw the graph based on the new values.

Let's add the following function just after the `drawGraph()` function:

```
$window.onresize = function() {
  scope.$apply(scope.drawGraph(scope.data));
};
```

We wrap our function with `scope.$apply()` to force `$digest` to rerun and update the values that have changed.

Refresh the page in the browser, and now try and resize the browser window; you'll notice something funny. The bars get drawn multiple times as the window is being resized. This is obviously because the `drawGraph` function is being called multiple times as the window is being dragged. We fix it is by first removing all items within the graph before we start drawing. We do this by adding one line of code in the `app/js/directives.js` file, as highlighted in the following code.

```
scope.drawGraph = function(data) {
  chart.selectAll('*').remove();
```

Adding touch events

Given that we are building this app mainly for mobile and tablet devices, it's crucial to allow touch and swipe events.

Enabling swipe gestures using ngTouch

Thankfully, AngularJS comes with a nice module called ngTouch, which allows us to easily add touch and swipe gestures. The ngTouch file doesn't come as a default with AngularJS and needs to be included separately.

Download the ngTouch file using bower by typing the following command in the terminal:

```
bower install angular-touch --save
```

We'll include ngTouch by adding the following script file in our `app/index.html` file, as highlighted in the following code:

```
<script src="bower_components/angular-touch/angular-touch.js"></script>
```

Make sure that ngTouch is called after AngularJS.

The next step is to add it as a dependency for our app.

We will add it in our `angular.module` function in our `app/js/app.js` file, as highlighted in the following code:

```
angular.module('myApp', [
  'ngRoute',
  'myApp.filters',
  'myApp.services',
  'myApp.directives',
  'myApp.controllers',
  'ngTouch'

])
```

The ngTouch module exposes the following three new event listeners.

- **ngClick**: This is an efficient event listener to detect mouse clicks and touch events
- **ngSwipeLeft**: This listener can be used to detect a swipe in the left direction
- **ngSwipeRight**: This listener can be used to detect a swipe in the right direction.

As we want swipe detection to be enabled around the whole app, we will write the code in the app/index.html file, as highlighted in the following code:

```
<body ng-swipe-left="goLeft()" ng-swipe-right="goRight()" ng-
controller="NavigationCtrl">
```

As you can see here, we call the goLeft() function on ng-swipe-left and the goRight() function on ng-swipe-right. We also define the NavigationCtrl controller within which we will define our goLeft and goRight functions.

Let's create our NavigationCrtl function within the app/js/controllers.js file as follows:

```
.controller('NavigationCtrl',['$scope' ,'$location',function($scope,$
location){
  var navigator = function(incrementer) {
    var pages = ['/', '/add-expense', '/view-summary'];

    var nextUrl = "";
    var currentPage = $location.path();
    var lastPageIndex = pages.length - 1;
    var pageIndex = pages.indexOf(currentPage);
    var direction = pageIndex + incrementer;
    if (direction === -1) direction = lastPageIndex;
    if (direction > lastPageIndex) direction = 0;
    nextUrl = pages[direction];
    $location.url(nextUrl);
  };
}])
```

We start by injecting the $location service into our controller. The navigator function, which we define next, is the crucial piece here.

The navigator function accepts an argument called incrementer which tells whether we want to move to the next page or the previous page. Within the navigator function, we first define a couple of items such as the pages array and the current page and the last page index.

Notice that we are making use of $location.path () to identify the current path and $location.url() to navigate to the new path.

Now, within out `NavigationCtrl` function, we will define our `goLeft` and `goRight` functions as follows:

```
$scope.goLeft = function() {
    navigator(-1);
};
$scope.goRight = function() {
    navigator(1);
};
```

Save the file, and run the page on the browser. Drag and release the mouse to the left and right to see the pages change.

Google Chrome, Firefox, and Safari come with excellent emulators to test and see how your app will look and perform on different form factors. You can also test it out on the iOS or Android simulators in case you have their SDKs installed.

Try the same from an actual device to see how the swipes work.

> Assuming that you are on a Wi-Fi network, you can simply type in the IP address of your local server in the address bar of the mobile to view the app.
>
> To know what is the IP address of your local server, open up the terminal and type in `ipconfig` if you are on Windows or `ifconfig` if you are on a Mac or Linux machine.

You might notice that at times, while swiping on the desktop or mobile screen, the background image starts to move. To prevent this from happening, we need to add a CSS property to the `.bg-image` class as follows:

```
.bg-image{ -webkit-user-drag: none;}
```

Note that this is in addition to the rest of the properties that are already present in the `bg-image` CSS class.

Adding page transitions using ngAnimate

Right now, the pages change abruptly when swiped upon; we would ideally like pages to slide in, to give it a more pleasant feel.

We will make use of the `ngAnimate` module to achieve our page transitions; it has been completely rewritten for Angular 1.2.x branches. It provides CSS3 transition and keyframe animation support for various AngularJS directives and controls.

Currently, the following directives support animations for enter and exit events:

- `ngView`
- `ngRepeat`
- `ngInclude`
- `ngIf`
- `ngSwitch`
- `ngClass`
- `ngShow`
- `ngHide`

The way `ngAnimate` works is it simply adds `ng-enter` and `ng-leave` CSS classes to the directive.

We are then required to write our own CSS3 transition effects for these classes. Let's see how to go about doing this.

Loading the ngAnimate module

Like `ngTouch`, even `ngAnimate` doesn't come by default with AngularJS, and it needs to be installed and included separately. First, run the following command in the terminal:

```
bower install angular-animate --save
```

We then include the `ngAnimate` JS file from the `lib` folder in the `app/index.html` file as follows:

```
<script src="bower_components/angular-animate/angular-animate.js"></script>
```

Next, we need to include it as a dependency to our app. We'll do so in the `app/js/app.js` file, as highlighted in the following code:

```
angular.module('myApp', [
  'ngRoute',
  'myApp.filters',
  'myApp.services',
  'myApp.directives',
  'myApp.controllers',
  'ngTouch',
  'ngAnimate'
])
```

Now, what we need to do is when the user swipes to the right, the pages move right, and on swiping to the left, the pages move left.

This means that we'll need to selectively add a CSS class depending on the swipe direction.

We do this using the `ng-class` directive in `ng-view`.

Update the `app/index.html` file as follows:

```
<div class="page-slide" ng-view ng-class="slidingDirection"></div>
```

Now, depending on the direction of the swipe, we will change the direction model.

For this, we will add a line to our navigator function in our `app/js/controllers.js` file:

```
$scope.slidingDirection = (incrementer === 1) ? 'slide-right' :
'slide-left';
```

Save the files, test it in the browser, and notice the `slide-left` and `slide-right` classes getting added to `ng-view`, depending on the direction of the swipe.

Adding CSS3 transitions

Now comes the part of adding in the CSS3 transition effects. Before we get to that, we'll first need to do some ground work by setting some basic style properties.

Add the `.page-slide` class in the `app/css/app.css` file as follows:

```
.page-slide {
  padding: 2% ;
  position: absolute;
  width: 85% ;
  min-height: 90% ;
  opacity: 0.8;
  background: #222;
  border: thin solid #111;
  margin: 0% 5% 5% ;
}
```

The important property here is `position:absolute`. As we are going to be animating the div's left property, it's necessary that we have the div set to `position absolute`.

Next, we set the transition parameters such as the duration of the transition, what all properties would be applied, and the easing of the transition.

```
.page-slide.ng-enter, .page-slide.ng-leave{
    transition: all 0.9s ease-out;
    -moz-transition: all 0.9s ease-out;
    -webkit-transition: all 0.9s ease-out;
}
```

On every change in view, `ngAnimate` will add four CSS classes to the div:

Class Name	Description
ng-enter	This is applied to the view that enters the screen. Properties that we set should define the starting point of our animation.
ng-enter-active	This is applied when the transition is in effect. The properties we set are for the end state of our animation.
ng-leave	This is applied when the view is exiting the screen. The properties that we apply are the starting point of the animation sequence.
ng-leave-active	This is applied during the transition. The properties applied are for the final state of the animation sequence.

Now, as our animations depend on the direction of the swipe, we will need to set two sets of classes. First, let's write the classes for the swipe-right effect.

We'll be doing this in the `app/css/app.css` file

```
.slide-right.ng-leave{
  left:0%;
}

.slide-right.ng-leave-active {
  left:100%;
}

.slide-right.ng-enter {
  left:-100%;
}
.slide-right.ng-enter-active {
  left:0%;
}
```

Save the file, and test the code by swiping to the right. As the old view slides out from the right-hand side, you should be able to see the new view slide in from the left-hand side.

On similar lines, we will add the classes for the swipe left.

```
.slide-left.ng-leave{
  left:0%;
}

.slide-left.ng-leave-active {
  left:-100%;
}

.slide-left.ng-enter {
  left:100%;
}
.slide-left.ng-enter-active {
  left:0%;
}
```

Making the app feel like a native app

One of the biggest problems with web apps is that as they need to be opened within the default browser, the browser's address bar and the next, previous, and bookmark buttons show up, giving the users a bad user experience.

Thankfully, we can make our app run in a fullscreen mode, but for this, the user needs to add the app to the home screen.

Adding touch icons

When the user adds the app to the home screen, it's important that we have an icon associated with it so that the users can easily identify the application.

This is where the touch icon comes into play.

We first need to create a touch icon for iOS devices using a graphic designing tool such as Photoshop or Gimp. As the iOS devices have different screen sizes and resolutions, we need to create a different icon for each size as per the following table.

All icons need to be saved in the PNG format; their sizes are given in the following table:

Device	Touch Icon Size
iPhone	60 px x 60 px
iPhone Retina	120 px x 120 px
iPad	76 px x 76 px
iPad Retina	152 px x 152 px

Once you have these icons created, place them in the root of our app folder and include them in the app/index.html file as follows:

```
<link rel="apple-touch-icon" href="touch-icon-iphone.png">
<link rel="apple-touch-icon" sizes="76x76" href="touch-icon-ipad.png">
<link rel="apple-touch-icon" sizes="120x120" href="touch-icon-iphone-
retina.png">
<link rel="apple-touch-icon" sizes="152x152" href="touch-icon-ipad-
retina.png">
```

Now, when we add the app to the home screen, we should see this icon being displayed. Clicking on this link will directly take us to the app.

Running the app in fullscreen mode

Although the icon from the home screen directly launches the app, we'll notice that the app still loads within the browser with the address bar and the next and back navigation buttons. In order to run the app in fullscreen mode, we need to add the following two meta tags to our app/index.html file as follows:

```
<meta name="mobile-web-app-capable" content="yes">
<meta name="apple-mobile-web-app-capable" content="yes">
```

This should now make our app feel more like a native app.

Adding additional features

This completes our chapter on building a mobile web app.

We can also convert this web app into a native app using tools such as PhoneGap. However, that would be beyond the scope of this book.

As an assignment, try adding in the following functionalities to the app:

- A delete button on the details grid that allows you to delete an individual expense item. You'll need to first identify the key of the selected item and then use the `localStorage.removeItem(key)` method to delete the item.

- A notification message box that displays a success or failure message while adding an expense. You can look to create your own directive to display the notification messages. Use Promises or try-catch blocks to identify if the data was saved or not.

Summary

In the course of this chapter, we saw how to use `localStorage` to store data persistently. We created our service factory that stores and retrieves data from `localStorage`. We also saw how to create SVG-based graphs using D3 and how to package it as a directive. We then went on to explore animations and touch events in AngularJS and how elegant sliding transitions can be built for swipe events. Finally, we saw how we can go about making our app feel like a native app by adding touch icons and opening the app in fullscreen mode.

In the next chapter, we will see how to build a full-fledged **Content Management System (CMS)** using AngularJS and the MEAN stack. See you on the other side.

7
Building a CMS on the MEAN Stack

As we begin this chapter, we are fairly comfortable with AngularJS and have built some interesting apps in our journey so far.

In this chapter, we will learn to build our own **Content Management System (CMS)**.

Until now, we have been heavily dependent on external web services to handle all our backend server-side work. Now, we will build our own backend using MongoDB, ExpressJS, AngularJS, and Node.js; all these together are also popularly known as the MEAN stack.

This chapter will focus more on making AngularJS work smoothly with a backend system.

As we get through this chapter, some of the interesting things that we'll learn are as follows:

- Building RESTful web services using Node.js and ExpressJS
- Saving and reading data from MongoDB
- Working with ExpressJS and AngularJS routes within the same application

Why the MEAN stack?

An obvious question would be why the choice of MongoDB, Node.js, and Express, when we could use any other stack.

To be politically correct, we could use any other technology, such as Java, PHP, ASP. NET, or even Ruby on Rails, to build the backend part of this project, and AngularJS would work just as fine.

The main reason to choose this stack is that all the tools within this stack use a single language, which is JavaScript. Other than this, each of the following tools offers certain unique benefits that make it equally suitable to build this application:

- **Node.js**: This is the most important tool in this stack. It allows us to build event-driven, nonblocking I/O applications using JavaScript. Thanks to Node.js, we are now able to write server-side applications in JavaScript.

- **ExpressJS**: This is a lightweight web application framework that allows us to build a server-side application on Node.js using the **Model View Controller (MVC)** design pattern.

- **MongoDB**: This is a very popular NoSQL database. It uses JavaScript to read and modify data, and the data is stored in the **Binary JSON (BSON)** format.

- **MongooseJS**: This is an object modeling tool for MongoDB. It provides a schema-based approach to model our data and also a much easier way to validate and query data in MongoDB.

Getting started with the MEAN stack

Let's start by installing the various tools that we'll need to build our application.

By this time, you probably already have Node.js installed and have become reasonably comfortable with starting and stopping the web servers.

As we proceed, take a moment to verify your current version of Node.js and upgrade it if necessary. The status of the latest version and how to upgrade it can be found on the Node.js site at `http://nodejs.org/`.

Setting up MongoDB

Depending on your operating system, MongoDB can be installed in multiple ways.

Perform the steps mentioned at the following links to install MongoDB on your operating system:

- **For Windows,** refer to `http://docs.mongodb.org/manual/tutorial/install-mongodb-on-windows/`

- **For Mac OS X,** refer to `http://docs.mongodb.org/manual/tutorial/install-mongodb-on-os-x/`

- **For Ubuntu,** refer to `http://docs.mongodb.org/manual/tutorial/install-mongodb-on-ubuntu/`

Once you have installed MongoDB, the next most important step is to create the folder to store your data.

Create an empty folder named `data/db` on the root using the following command line:

```
mkdir /data/db
```

You can also create the folder directly in the `c:` as follows:

```
c:\md data
c:\md data\db
```

Next, we'll connect to the MongoDB database using the following command:

```
mongod
```

 You will need to either give read or write permissions to the `data/db` folder or use the `sudo` or `admin` privilege to run the MongoDB command with root-level privileges.

In the following steps, we will start the mongo shell and create a new database named `angcms`.

With MongoDB running in a terminal window, we will open a new terminal window and fire the following commands.

```
mongo
use angcms
```

MongoDB comes with a default `test` database; one can also use this to test and play around with some MongoDB commands.

Setting up ExpressJS and MongooseJS

In case you don't have ExpressJS yet, you can install it using the following command:

```
npm install -g express-generator
```

The next step is to create your ExpressJS project folder, which will be done using the following command:

```
express angcms
```

This will create a folder named `angcms` and put the boilerplate Express files into it. Note that we still don't have ExpressJS installed; we will need to install it with the following command from the terminal:

```
npm install
```

We'll now install MongooseJS as a devdependency along with ExpressJS.

Save the file, `cd`, into the `angcms` folder, and run the following command:

```
npm install --save mongoose
```

Go to the `angcms/node_modules` folder, and verify that we have the `express`, `jade`, and `mongoose` folders within it.

Let's also check whether our server is working by firing the following command in the terminal:

```
npm start
```

Open the browser and run `http://localhost:3000`; you should get the **Welcome to Express** message.

Building the server-side app

We'll start by building the server-side section of the app. We'll build a series of routes that will provide **Create**, **Read**, **Update**, **Delete** (**CRUD**) operations on our MongoDB database. We will expose these as REST APIs.

Let's write our models and custom routes into a separate route file to keep things clean.

Creating the Mongoose schemas

We first start by loading the `mongoose` library and establishing a connection to the `angcms` database. We add the following highlighted code in the `angcms/app.js` file:

```
var app = express();
var mongoose = require('mongoose');
mongoose.connect('mongodb://localhost/angcms');
var db = mongoose.connecetion;
```

For this application, we are going to need two schemas: the Pages schema and the Admin Users schema. Let's create these now.

We'll create a new folder named `models`, and create our `page.js` file with the following code in it:

```
var mongoose = require('mongoose');
var Schema = mongoose.Schema;
    var Page = new Schema({
        title: String,
        url: {type:String, index:{unique:true}},
        content: String,
        menuIndex: Number,
        date: Date     });
    var Page = mongoose.model('Page', Page);
    module.exports=Page;
```

The following table gives a description for the fields in the schema:

Fields	Description
title	The title of the content page.
url	The SEO-friendly alias that will be used to identify the page. Note that we are setting its index to `unique` as we don't want duplicate URL aliases.
content	The content of the page.
menuIndex	An integer that defines the menu sequence of the pages in the navigation bar.
date	The date when this document was last updated.

Next, we create the schema for our admin users in the `models/admin-users.js` file as follows:

```
var mongoose = require('mongoose');
var Schema = mongoose.Schema;
var adminUser = new Schema({
        username: String,
        password: String
    });
    var adminUser = mongoose.model('adminUser', adminUser);

module.exports=adminUser;
```

As you can see, we are keeping things very simple, with our admin user's schema only storing the username and password.

Creating CRUD routes

Now, we'll start writing the routes for the CRUD operations; we'll start by generating the listing page.

Create a new file, `routes/api.js`, in the `routes` folder, and add the following code:

```
var express = require('express');
var router = express.Router();
var mongoose = require('mongoose');
var Page= require('../models/page.js');
var adminUser= require('../models/admin-users.js');

/* User Routes. */

router.get('/', function(req, res) {
  res.send('Welcome to the API zone');
});

router.get('/pages', function(request, response) {

        return Page.find(function(err, pages) {
            if (!err) {
                return response.send(pages);
            } else {
                return response.send(500, err);
            }
        });
    });

module.exports = router;
```

What the preceding code does is that it runs the `find()` method on the `Page` schema and returns the list of pages found. In case of an error, it would return a status code of **500** and display the error message. We need to get back to our `app.js` file and add the following lines to create
these routes:

```
var api = require('./routes/api');

app.use('/api', api);
```

Add the preceding two lines within the respective sections of the app.js file.

Make sure that app.use('/api', api); is called before app.use('/', routes);. This will ensure that the /api routes get higher priority than the others.

On the terminal, stop and restart the npm using the npm start command. Note that you need to restart the web server every time you make a change to the server-side code.

On the browser, navigate to http://localhost:3000/api/pages.

You should see empty square brackets. This means that our current collection is empty.

Adding a new entry to the collection

Next, let's write the route to add data to our collection. We will continue adding it to the routes/api.js file as follows:

```
router.post('/pages/add', function(request, response) {
    var page = new Page({
        title: request.body.title,
        url: request.body.url,
        content: request.body.content,
        menuIndex: request.body.menuIndex,
        date: new Date(Date.now())
    });

    page.save(function(err) {
        if (!err) {
            return response.send(200, page);

        } else {
            return response.send(500,err);
        }
    });
});
```

As we need to pass data to our server script, we will use the post method instead of get. Next, we create a new instance of our page object and pass the request parameters from our post data. We then call the save method, which does the actual task of saving this data into the collection.

We can test this route by simulating the `post` action using either the browser's developer tools console or Firebug console. Alternatively, there are quite a few REST clients available as browser extensions and add-ons that can help you simulate the `post` action.

Try to create a couple of pages using this method, and run http://localhost:3000/api/pages to verify that this data is being saved and returned as a JSON response. You'll also notice an additional key named `_id` being saved along with each of these nodes. We will be using the `_id` key for our delete and update operations

Updating a collection

Once we have the route to save a new entry, the next logical step is to create our route that will allow us to update an entry. We'll continue to write the code to modify a collection item in our `angcms/routes/api.js` file as follows:

```
router.post('/pages/update', function(request, response) {
    var id = request.body._id;

    Page.update({
        _id: id
    }, {
        $set: {
            title: request.body.title,
            url: request.body.url,
            content: request.body.content,
            menuIndex: request.body.menuIndex,
            date: new Date(Date.now())
        }
    }).exec();
    response.send("Page updated");
});
```

Deleting a collection item

Next comes the route to delete an item; while continuing to work on the same file, we add the following code:

```
router.get('/pages/delete/:id', function(request, response) {
    var id = request.params.id;
    Page.remove({
        _id: id
    }, function(err) {
        return console.log(err);
```

```
        });
        return response.send('Page id- ' + id + ' has been deleted');
    });
```

Ensure that the code is working by testing it with a REST client or typing in the route URL in a browser window along with a valid ID.

Displaying a single record

Next, we will write the route to fetch the data for an individual page on the admin side.

We'll continue by adding the following code to our api.js file:

```
    router.get('/pages/admin-details/:id', function(request, response) {
        var id = request.params.id;
        Page.findOne({
            _id: id
        }, function(err, page) {
            if (err)
                return console.log(err);
            return response.send(page);
        });
    });
```

We use the get method here and pass the ID as a request parameter. We then run the findOne method to pull up a single record that matches the ID and return that as a response.

You can easily verify this route by simply appending the ID to the URL endpoint as follows:

http://localhst:3000/api/pages/view/<_id>.

On similar lines, we will also create another route to fetch the page contents for the frontend. Here, in the following code, we will use the URL as a parameter to fetch the data because we would like our frontend to show SEO-friendly URLs:

```
    router.get('/pages/details/:url', function(request, response) {
        var url = request.params.url;
        Page.findOne({
            url: url
        }, function(err, page) {
            if (err)
                return console.log(err);
            return response.send(page);
        });
    });
```

Securing your admin section

Now, it's time to secure the admin section so that only authorized users can log in.

An important thing to note here is that we will need to secure both the client-side admin section and also our server-side APIs, because it is relatively easy to bypass client-side validations.

We will start with securing our server-side code. ExpressJS comes with its own session management and encryption modules.

We will enable `cookieParser` in our app by adding the following line to our `angcms/app.js` file:

```
app.use(express.cookieParser('secret'));
```

Using bcrypt to encrypt passwords

To encrypt confidential data such as passwords, we will use a popular utility called **bcrypt** to hash the password before it is stored in the database.

Let's download and install the `bcrypt-nodejs` package using the following terminal command from the root of the project folder:

```
npm install bcrypt-nodejs
```

Next, we will include this in our ExpressJS app. As we will be securing our routes, we'll include the `bcrypt` module in our `angcms/routes/api.js` file as follows:

```
var bcrypt = require('bcrypt-nodejs');
```

Adding a new admin user

Along with this, we will create our route to add in a new admin user as follows:

```
router.post('/add-user', function(request, response) {
    var salt, hash, password;
    password = request.body.password;
    salt = bcrypt.genSaltSync(10);
    hash = bcrypt.hashSync(password, salt);

    var AdminUser = new adminUser({
        username: request.body.username,
        password: hash
    });
```

```
AdminUser.save(function(err) {
    if (!err) {
        return response.send('Admin User successfully created');

    } else {
        return response.send(err);
    }
});
});
```

Here, we first start by defining our `password`, `salt`, and `hash` variables.

Then, using `bcrypt` and `salt`, we generate the `hash` string of the password.

 Using the `salt` variable is optional with `bcrypt`, but it is recommended, as it makes it difficult for potential hackers to decrypt the hashed password.

We then create a new instance of the `AdminUser` object, store the username and hashed password, and run the save method to save this information in the `AdminUser` document in MongoDB.

Creating the route for authenticating login

Next, we create the route for login. Add the following code to the `api.js` file:

```
router.post('/login', function(request, response) {
  var username = request.body.username;
  var password = request.body.password;

  adminUser.findOne({
    username: username
  }, function(err, data) {
    if (err | data === null) {
      return response.send(401, "User Doesn't exist");
    } else {
      var usr = data;

      if (username == usr.username && bcrypt.compareSync(password,
        usr.password)) {

        request.session.regenerate(function() {
          request.session.user = username;
          return response.send(username);
```

```
        });
    } else {
        return response.send(401, "Bad Username or Password");
    }
    }
    });
});
```

The code piece, although long, is fairly straightforward.

We capture the username and password as variables from the post data. We then check to see if the username is present, and if it is, then using the compare method of bcrypt, we check to see if the password entered matches that stored in the database.

Once the username and password match, we create the user session and redirect the user to the page's listing page.

In case the username or password doesn't exist, we return back with a status code 401 and a relevant error message.

We will be using this status code in our AngularJS side to redirect the users in case of session time outs and so on.

Creating the logout route

After the login function, we create the logout function as follows:

```
router.get('/logout', function(request, response) {
    request.session.destroy(function() {
        return response.send(401, 'User logged out');

    });
});
```

The function will simply destroy the session.

Writing the sessionCheck middleware

The next step is to create our middleware function that does a session check.

As of ExpressJS Version 4.x, all the middleware, except static, have been removed and need to be installed and included as needed. Thus, we download our session module with the following terminal command:

```
npm install express-session --save
```

We then include the following lines in the respective sections of our app.js file:

```
var session = require('express-session');
app.use (session());
```

Next, we write our function that will check the user sessions. We add this to the api.js file:

```
function sessionCheck(request,response,next){

    if(request.session.user) next();
        else response.send(401,'authorization failed');
}
```

Now, to secure the API routes, we simply need to call the sessionCheck function after the route name, as highlighted in the following code:

```
router.post('/pages/add', sessionCheck, function(request,
  response) {
```

Usually, we'd want to secure the APIs that modify the data, and hence, we will add the sessionCheck function to the add, update, and delete APIs as follows:

- For the update API, it should be as follows:

```
router.post('/pages/update', sessionCheck, function(request,
response) {
```

- For the delete API, it should be as follows::

```
router.get ('/pages/delete/:id', sessionCheck,
function(request,response){
```

- For the details API, it should be as follows::

```
router.get('/pages/admin-details/:id', sessionCheck,
function(request, response) {
```

Integrating AngularJS with an ExpressJS project

Now that we have most of our server-side code working, we'll start working on our AngularJS code.

Let's download the angular-seed project as a ZIP download from https://github.com/areai51/angular-seed and extract the contents of the ZIP file.

Now, we will only take the content of the app folder along with the `package.json` and `bower.json` files and place it within the `public` folder of angcms.

In the terminal, navigate to the `angcms/public` folder and run the following two commands:

```
npm install
bower install
```

Note that we do not run `npm start` from within the `public` folder, as we will be using the Express server that runs at port 3000.

Your folder structure should look something like the following:

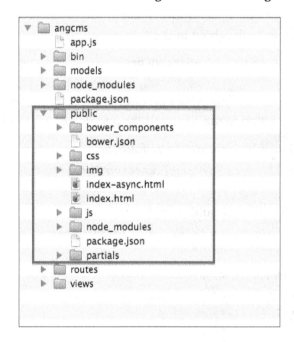

The next step is to define the routes in our ExpressJS app such that all routes are managed by AngularJS, except for those that start with a`/api/`.

For this, we will add the following catch-all route at the end of the `angcms/routes/index.js` file as follows:

```
router.get('*', function(request, response) {
    response.sendfile('./public/index.html');
});
```

The routes in ExpressJS are executed sequentially, and hence, the catch-all route needs to be at the end.

Restart your `app.js` node application and point the browser URL to `http://localhost:3000/index.html`. Verify that the page displayed is the default `index.html` file of `angular-seed`.

Generating SEO-friendly URLs using HTML5 mode

All this while, all the URLs in our AngularJS app have had # in the URLs. When building a CMS, ensuring that the URLs are meaningful and SEO-friendly is quite important.

To make our site URLs are SEO friendly, we need to turn on the HTML5 mode in `$locationProvider` by making the following highlighted changes in the `angcms/public/js/app.js` file:

```
.config(['$routeProvider', '$locationProvider',
    function($routeProvider, $locationProvider) {
  $routeProvider.when('/view1', {templateUrl:
    'partials/partial1.html', controller: 'MyCtrl1'});
  $routeProvider.when('/view2', {templateUrl:
    'partials/partial2.html', controller: 'MyCtrl2'});
  $routeProvider.otherwise({redirectTo: '/view1'});
  $locationProvider.html5Mode(true);
}]);
```

The next thing to do is set the base URL in our `angcms/public/index.html` file, as highlighted in the following code:

```
<title>AngCMS</title>
    <base href="/">
  <link rel="stylesheet" href="css/bootstrap.min.css"/>
```

Refresh the **Index** page, and you will notice that your URLs are now clean without the # symbol in them.

Building the admin section for CRUD operations

We will now look to build the admin section of our CMS using Angular JS. The AngularJS app will talk to the backend ExpressJS scripts that we just wrote in the preceding section.

Creating the routes for the admin section

Ideally, we would like our admin section to be called from within the admin URL, so let's go ahead and add the routes for the admin section of the AngularJS app.

Add the following routes to the angcms/public/js/app.js file:

```
config(['$routeProvider', '$locationProvider',
    function($routeProvider, $locationProvider) {

        $routeProvider.when('/admin/login', {
            templateUrl: 'partials/admin/login.html',
            controller: 'AdminLoginCtrl'
        });
        $routeProvider.when('/admin/pages', {
            templateUrl: 'partials/admin/pages.html',
            controller: 'AdminPagesCtrl'
        });
        $routeProvider.when('/admin/add-edit-page/:id', {
            templateUrl: 'partials/admin/add-edit-page.html',
            controller: 'AddEditPageCtrl'
        });
        $routeProvider.otherwise({
            redirectTo: '/'
        });
        $locationProvider.html5Mode(true);
    }
]);
```

For the admin side, we have three routes: /admin/login is to authenticate the user, /admin/pages will show the list of pages available, and /admin/add-edit-page/:id will be used to add or edit the contents of the page. Note that we will make use of a single route to both add and edit a page.

Building the factory services

As we are going to be reading the dynamic data from web services, we will create a factory service that will be used to communicate with the backend web service.

Let's create our factory web services that will do the CRUD operations.

We will add the following methods to our `angcms/public/js/services.js` file:

```
'use strict';
angular.module('myApp.services', [])

.factory('pagesFactory', ['$http',
  function($http) {

    return {
      getPages: function() {
        return $http.get('/api/pages');
      },

      savePage: function(pageData) {
        var id = pageData._id;

        if (id === 0) {
          return $http.post('/api/pages/add', pageData);
        } else {
          return $http.post('/api/pages/update', pageData);
        }
      },
      deletePage: function(id) {
        return $http.get('/api/pages/delete/' + id);
      },
      getAdminPageContent: function(id) {
        return $http.get('/api/pages/admin-details/' + id);
      },
      getPageContent: function(url) {
        return $http.get('/api/pages/details/' + url);
      },
    };
  }
]);
```

The methods to list, delete, and view the details of a page are quite straightforward; we simply make a request to the appropriate ExpressJS route that passes the `id` parameter where necessary.

Focusing on the `savePage` method, you'll notice that we are using the same method to add a new page or edit the contents of an existing page. What we do here is we check for the `id` value in our `post` data. If the `id` value is set to `0`, then it is treated as adding a new record; otherwise, it will try to update the record whose `id` value is being passed.

Building the controllers for the admin section

Now that we have our factory services ready, we'll get started with writing our controllers.

We'll add the following code to the `angcms/public/js/controllers.js` file:

```
'use strict';
angular.module('myApp.controllers', []).
  controller('AdminPagesCtrl', ['$scope', '$log', 'pagesFactory',
    function($scope, $log, pagesFactory) {
      pagesFactory.getPages().then(
        function(response) {
          $scope.allPages = response.data;
        },
        function(err) {
          $log.error(err);
        });

      $scope.deletePage = function(id) {
        pagesFactory.deletePage(id);
      };


    }
]);
```

 Don't forget to delete the default controllers that come as a part of the `angular-seed` package.

The `AdminPagesCtrl` controller is primarily used to display the page's listing.

We make a request to the `getPages` method of `pagesFactory` and populate the `allPages` scope object using the promise.

We also define our method to delete a page; the method accepts the `id` value as an input parameter.

Setting up the admin page layout

We'll now work on building our listing view that will display a list of all the pages, along with the ability to add, edit, or delete a page.

Before we get to our listing view, let's first get the groundwork ready on our **Index** page located at `angcms/public/index.html`.

Ensure that your `index.html` file contains the following code:

```
<!doctype html>
<html lang="en" ng-app="myApp">

<head>
    <meta charset="utf-8">
    <title>Angular CMS</title>
     <base href="/">
    <link rel="stylesheet" href="bower_components/bootstrap/dist/css/
     bootstrap.min.css" />
    <link rel="stylesheet" href="bower_components/bootstrap/dist/css/
     bootstrap-theme.min.css" />
    <link rel="stylesheet" href="css/app.css" />
</head>

<body>
    <div class="container" ng-view></div>
    <script src="bower_components/angular/angular.js"></script>
    <script src="bower_components/angular-route/angular-route.js"></
script>
   <script src="js/app.js"></script>
    <script src="js/services.js"></script>
    <script src="js/controllers.js"></script>
    <script src="js/filters.js"></script>
    <script src="js/directives.js"></script>
</body>

</html>
```

We will leverage BootStrap3 to get our styling in place. You can choose to either download Bootstrap from `www.getbootstrap.com`, call it from any of the CDN, or run the following command in the terminal from within the `angcms/public` folder:

bower install bootstrap

As you can see from the code, we are loading `bootstrap` and Bootstrap-theme CSS files to take advantage of the default Bootstrap theme.

The only other change to the `index.html` file at this stage is adding the `container` CSS class to our `ng-view` div. This will act as the container for all the pages that load within it.

Building the listing view for the admin section

Next, we'll create the partial that will display our list of pages stored in the database.

Create a folder named `admin` and a new file named `pages.html` at `angcms/public/partials/admin/pages.html`, and add the following code:

```
<a href="#/admin/add-edit-page/0" class="btn btn-success
    pull-right"> Add New Page</a>
<h1>Pages List</h1>
<hr/>
<table class="table">
  <thead>
    <tr>
      <th>Menu Index</th>
      <th>Title</th>
      <th>URL</th>
      <th>Edit</th>
      <th>Delete</th>
    </tr>
  </thead>

  <tr ng-repeat="page in allPages">
    <td>{{page.menuIndex}}</td>
    <td>{{page.title}}</td>
    <td>{{page.url}}</td>
    <td> <a ng-href="#/admin/add-edit-page/{{page._id}}">Edit</a>
    </td>
    <td> <a ng-href="#" ng-click="deletePage(page._id)">Delete</a>
    </td>
  </tr>
</table>
```

At the top, we have a button to add new pages. It will link to the `add-edit-page` route and pass a fixed ID of `0`. As you might have realized, we are reusing our partial to add and edit the page. We will need to let AngularJS know when to call the `add` endpoint and when to call the `edit` endpoint. For this reason, we pass `0` as a parameter while adding a new page and the MongoDB-assigned ID while editing a page.

The next piece of code is the table to display our list of pages with the title and URL fields. Along with it, we also have links to edit or delete the respective page. Both these hyperlinks link to the respective routes that pass the page ID.

Save the file and point the browser URL to `http://localhost:3000/admin/pages`. This should show you a list of pages. In case you don't see any pages, check for any console errors or add some content using a REST Client for the time being, until our `add-edit-page` route is ready.

The delete link will not work for now as its API is authenticated.

Setting up authentication in AngularJS

Before we can proceed to build the client-side sections, we'll need to build the login and session management modules in AngularJS. We'll need to do this now, because the rest of the services for the CRUD operation are secured on the server side.

Creating our login page

We will start with the creation of our partial by creating a new file in `angcms/public/partials/admin/login.html`, and we will put in the following code:

```
<h1>Login</h1>
<hr/>

<form role="form" id="login" ng-submit="login(credentials)">

<div class="form-group">
<label>Login</label>

<input class="form-control" type="text" ng-model="credentials.
username"/>
</div>
<div class="form-group">
<label>Password</label>
<input class="form-control" type="password"  ng-model="
  credentials.password"/>
</div>

<input type="submit" class="btn btn-success" value="Login">
</div>
</form>
```

Next, we will create our controller in the `angcms/public/js/controllers.js` file with the following code.

```
.controller('AdminLoginCtrl', ['$scope', '$location',
  '$cookies', 'AuthService','$log',
    function($scope, $location, $cookies, AuthService, $log) {
```

```
            $scope.credentials = {
              username: '',
              password: ''
            };
            $scope.login = function(credentials) {
              AuthService.login(credentials).then(
                function(res, err) {
                  $cookies.loggedInUser = res.data;
                  $location.path('/admin/pages');
                },
                function(err) {
                  $log.log(err);
                });
            };
        }
    ])
```

You'll notice that we have injected $location, AuthService, $scope, $log, and $cookies into our controller function.

AngularJS has a module called ngCookies that allows to read and write to the browser cookie. However, this doesn't come as a part of the AngularJS library and needs to be included separately.

Run the following command in the terminal to download angular-cookies:

```
bower install angular-cookies
```

We'll first need to load the angular-cookies.js file in our angcms/public/index.html file as follows:

```
<script type="text/javascript" src="bower_components/angular-cookies/
    angular-cookies.js"></script>
```

Next, we need to include the ngCookies module as a part of our main application. We do this in our angcms/public/js/app.js file, as highlighted in the following code:

```
angular.module('myApp', [
    'ngRoute',
    'myApp.filters',
    'myApp.services',
    'myApp.directives',
    'myApp.controllers',
    'ngCookies'
])
```

Next, we will create the `AuthService` factory that will contain the login and logout methods. Add the following code in the `angcms/public/js/services.js` file:

```
.factory('AuthService', ['$http', function($http) {
  return {
    login: function(credentials) {
      return $http.post('/api/login', credentials);
    },
    logout: function() {
      return $http.get('/api/logout');
    }
  };
}])
```

Let's test our login functionality. Open the following URL in the browser, and log in with the correct username and password:

`http://localhost:3000/admin/login`

Using the correct username and password, you should get redirected to the pages listing.

> Make sure you have a couple of admin users saved; if not, use a REST API Client and create a couple of admin users using the following API URL:
>
> `http://localhost:3000/api/add-user`

Building a custom module for global notification

As you might have realized by now, our login page works fine as long as we put the correct credentials; however, when you try with an invalid username or password, the page doesn't do anything.

> The developer console should, however, show a **401 Unauthorized** failed message.

We will need to build a notification system that displays a message when invalid credentials are passed. Thinking a few steps ahead, you'll realize that we are going to need such messages displayed on many occasions, for example, when a new page has been created or updated, or when a page has been deleted.

In view of this, it is most ideal to build a global notification system that can be used all throughout our application.

AngularJS allows us to create custom modules. These are self-contained modules that can be easily reused across multiple applications. A custom module is simply a wrapper that holds different parts of an AngularJS app; these parts can be directives, services, filters, controllers, and so on.

As you would recall, `ngCookies` is a similar custom module we just made use of earlier.

Building and initializing the message.flash module

We will create a new file named `message-flash.js` at `angcms/public/js/message-flash.js`.

We will initialize it with the following code:

```
angular.module('message.flash', [])
```

We also need to include this in our app, so let's include the `message-flash.js` file in our `angcms/public/index.html` file, as follows:

```
<script src="js/message-flash.js"></script>
```

Next, we add the `message-flash.js` file as a dependency in our main module in the `angcms/public/js/app.js` file, as highlighted in the following code:

```
angular.module('myApp', [
    'ngRoute',
    'myApp.filters',
    'myApp.services',
    'myApp.directives',
    'myApp.controllers',
    'ui.tinymce',
    'ngCookies',
    'message.flash'
])
```

Building the message.flash factory service

We will chain our factory to the message.flash module in our angcms/public/js/ message-flash.js file, as highlighted in the following code:

```
angular.module('message.flash', [])
.factory('flashMessageService', ['$rootScope',function($rootScope) {
  var message = '';
  return {
    getMessage: function() {
      return message;
    },
    setMessage: function(newMessage) {
      message = newMessage;
    }
  };
}])
```

The factory service is quite straightforward. We initialize a variable called message and have two methods, namely, setMessage and getMessage, which assign and read values to the message variable.

Setting up $broadcasts

Anybody who has tried to pass variables from one controller to another or to a directive would have realized that it isn't quite straightforward, and one needs to use either rootScope or set up $watch or $digest to ensure that the scope objects update when the source has changed.

We will face a similar problem here where the message in our directive wouldn't update when we pass the message from a controller.

To overcome this, we will set up $broadcast.

The broadcast, $broadcast, dispatches an event name to all child scopes. Child scopes use this as a trigger to execute different functions.

In our case, as we don't really have a parent-child relation between the directive and our controllers, we will set up a broadcast on rootScope itself

We add the broadcast event to the `setMessage` method in the `message-flash.js` file as highlighted:

```
setMessage: function(newMessage) {
  message=newMessage;
  $rootScope.$broadcast('NEW_MESSAGE')
}
```

Now, every time the `setMessage` function is called, we will broadcast the event called `'NEW_MESSAGE'`.

Building the directive for the message.flash module

We will continue to chain our directive to the same module in the `message-flash.js` file as follows:

```
.directive('messageFlash', [function() {
  return {
    controller: function($scope, flashMessageService, $timeout) {
      $scope.$on('NEW_MESSAGE', function() {
        $scope.message = flashMessageService.getMessage();
        $scope.isVisible = true;
        return $timeout(function() {
          $scope.isVisible = false;
          return $scope.message = '';
        }, 2500);
      })
    },
    template: '<p ng-if="isVisible" class="alert
      alert-info">{{message}}</p>'
  }
 }
]);
```

The directive code is quite interesting. We first listen for the broadcast event, and on its trigger, we populate `$scope.message` by calling the `getMessage` function of `flashMessageService`.

It is usually a good usability practice to hide the flash message after a few seconds of being visible; hence, we will add a timeout function that will automatically hide the message in `2500` milliseconds.

The last piece of code of the directive is the template code that uses the `ng-if` directive to toggle the display. We also use Bootstrap's alert CSS classes for some visual elegance.

Now, let's add this directive to our main `index.html` file, as highlighted in the following code:

```
<div message-flash> </div>
  <div  class="container" ng-view></div>
```

Setting a flash message

Let's revisit our `AdminLoginCtrl` function and set a flash message in case the login fails.

We add it to our `controller.js` file, as highlighted.

```
.controller('AdminLoginCtrl', ['$scope', '$location',
   '$cookies', 'AuthService', 'flashMessageService',function(
      $scope, $location, $cookies, AuthService,
         flashMessageService) {
         $scope.credentials = {
           username: '',
           password: ''
         };
         $scope.login = function(credentials) {

           AuthService.login(credentials).then(
             function(res, err) {
               $cookies.loggedInUser = res.data;
               $location.path('/admin/pages');

             },
             function(err) {
               flashMessageService.setMessage(err.data);

               console.log(err);

           });
         };
      }
   ])
```

Let's test our login page with an invalid username and password, and we should be able to see our flash message.

Creating our Add-Edit page controller

Now that we have our global messaging system in place, let's continue with building the rest of the admin sections

We'll start to create our controller for adding and editing pages.

Create a new controller function in the `angcms/public/controllers.js` file as follows:

```
.controller('AddEditPageCtrl', ['$scope', '$log', 'pagesFactory',
  '$routeParams', '$location', 'flashMessageService',
    function($scope, $log, pagesFactory, $routeParams,
      $location, flashMessageService) {
        $scope.pageContent = {};
        $scope.pageContent._id = $routeParams.id;
        $scope.heading = "Add a New Page";

        if ($scope.pageContent._id !== 0) {
          $scope.heading = "Update Page";
          pagesFactory.getAdminPageContent(
            $scope.pageContent._id).then(
              function(response) {
                $scope.pageContent = response.data;
                $log.info($scope.pageContent);
              },
              function(err) {
                $log.error(err);
              });
        }

        $scope.savePage = function() {
          pagesFactory.savePage($scope.pageContent).then(
            function() {
              flashMessageService.setMessage("Page Saved
                Successfully");
              $location.path('/admin/pages');
            },
            function() {
              $log.error('error saving data');
            }
          );
        };
    }
])
```

We start by defining our `AddEditPageCtrl` controller and injecting the necessary dependencies. Besides `$scope` and `$log`, we need to inject `$routeparams` to get the route parameters, the `$location` module to redirect, `flashMessageService` to set notifications, and `pagesFactory` service.

Next, we check to see if the page ID being passed is 0; this corresponds to an insert or the long MongoDB-generated ID, which means we'll be doing an update.

In case if it's the MongoDB-generated ID, we then need to fetch the data of the page and populate the edit template. For this, we make a call to the `getPageContent` factory function, and using promises, we populate our `pageContent` scope with the returned data.

The next part is writing the `savePage` function, which will save the contents of the form by posting it to the `savePage` factory function. When the promise returns with a success, we redirect the user back to the listing page.

Creating our Add-Edit view

Now that we have the controller in place, let's work on the form to add and edit the page content.

Create a new file at `angcms/public/partials/add-edit-page.html`, and add the following content:

```html
<h1>{{heading}}</h1>
<hr/>

<form role="form" id="add-page" ng-submit="savePage()">
<div class="form-group">
<label>Page ID</label>
<input class="form-control" type="text" readonly
    ng-model="pageContent._id"/>
</div>
<div class="form-group">
<label>Page Title</label>

<input class="form-control" type="text"
    ng-model="pageContent.title"/>
</div>
<div class="form-group">
<label>Page URL Alias</label>
<input class="form-control"type="text"
  ng-model="pageContent.url"/>
</div>
```

```
<div class="form-group">
<label>Menu Index</label>
<input class="form-control"type="number"
  ng-model="pageContent.menuIndex"/>
</div>

<div class="form-group">
<label>Page Content</label>
<textarea rows="15" class="form-control" type="text"
  ng-model="pageContent.content"></textarea>
</div>
<input type="submit" class="btn btn-success" value="Save">
</div>
</form>
```

Test the add page to ensure that it's working.

Writing a custom filter to autogenerate the URL field

Most CMS tools would autogenerate the URL alias based on the title of the page. While doing this, we will need to ensure that the alias being generated is stripped out of any special characters and all spaces are ideally replaced by a dash.

We will do this by creating our own custom filter.

Open up the `angcms/public/js/filters.js` file, and add the following code.

```
'use strict';

/* Filters */

angular.module('myApp.filters', [])
  .filter('formatURL', [
    function() {
      return function(input) {
        var url = input.replace(/[`~!@#$%^&*()_|+\-=?;:'",.<>\
          {\}\[\]\\\/]/gi, '');
        var url = url.replace(/[\s+]/g, '-');
        return url.toLowerCase();

      };
    }
  ]);
```

Here, we are basically creating a filter called `formatURL` and taking in the input parameters. We first remove any special characters that may be present using regex. We then replace all spaces with a hyphen and return the formatted string in lowercase.

Now, let's see how to use it in our code. We will use this filter in our controller, so let's make the highlighted changes in our controller file located at `angcms/public/js/controlllers.js`:

```
.controller('AddEditPageCtrl', ['$scope', '$log', 'pagesFactory',
    '$routeParams', '$location', 'flashMessageService','$filter',
    function($scope, $log, pagesFactory, $routeParams, $location,
        flashMessageService,$filter) {
```

As you can see, we are injecting the `$filter` module into our controller.

Next, we create a `$scope` function as follows:

```
$scope.updateURL=function(){
  $scope.pageContent.url=$filter('formatURL')($scope.pageContent.
title);
  }
```

Within the update URL function, we store the value into the `pageContent.url` property by using the `formatURL` filter and passing `$scope.pageContent.title` as an argument to it.

Next, we need to make the highlighted changes to our partial located at `angcms/public/partials/admin/add-edit-page.html`, as highlighted:

```
<label>Page Title</label>
<input class="form-control" type="text" ng-change="updateURL()" ng-
model="pageContent.title"/>
</div>
<div class="form-group">
<label>Page URL Alias</label>
<input class="form-control"type="text" readonly ng-model="pageContent.
url"/>
</div>
```

Save the files and test the add-edit page in the browser. Notice the URL field getting updated automatically as you enter the title field.

Adding the WYSIWYG editor

Most CMS tools would have a **What You See Is What You Get (WYSIWYG)** editor. This allows the content administrators to easily format the text on a page, for example, add headings, make the text bold or italics, add numbering bullets, and so on.

We'll see how to add **TinyMCE**, a very popular WYSIWYG editor, to our page content text area.

Angular UI has a ready-to-use module, which makes it very easy to add TinyMCE to any form in an AngularJS app.

The Angular-UI TinyMCE wrapper can be downloaded from GitHub at `https://github.com/angular-ui/ui-tinymce`.

Alternatively, we can also use bower to download the files.

Assuming that you have already installed bower, run the following command in the terminal;

```
bower install angular-ui-tinymce --save
```

This will create a folder called `bower_components` and download the files within it.

Next, let's include these libraries in our `index.html` file, as highlighted in the following code:

```
<script type="text/javascript" src="bower_components/tinymce/
    tinymce.min.js"></script>
<script type="text/javascript" src="lib/angular/
    angular.js"></script>
<script type="text/javascript" src="bower_components/
    angular-ui-tinymce/src/tinymce.js"></script>
<script src="lib/angular/angular-route.js"></script>
```

Next, we will add the TinyMCE module as a dependency to our app in the `angcms/public/js/app.js` file, as highlighted in the following code:

```
angular.module('myApp', [
    'ngRoute',
    'myApp.filters',
    'myApp.services',
    'myApp.directives',
    'myApp.controllers',
    'ui.tinymce',
    'ngCookies',
    'message.flash'
]).
```

This is all that is required to include TinyMCE in our AngularJS app.

Now, to add the editor to our `angcms/public/partials/admin/add-edit-page.html` file, we will simply call our directive, as highlighted in the following code:

```
<textarea ui-tinymce rows="15" class="form-control"
    type="text" ng-model="pageContent.content"></textarea>
```

Save the file, and now, try to add or edit a page to notice TinyMCE replace the text area.

Setting up an Interceptor to detect responses

A use case that we need to consider is what happens if the backend web service's session timed out and somebody from the frontend is trying to add, edit, or delete a page.

At the instance when the backend service times out, it would return a 401 status code; we would need to have every AngularJS controller check for this status code and redirect the user to the login page in case it gets one.

Instead of writing this check on each and every controller, we will make use of an **Interceptor** to check every incoming response, and act accordingly.

Let's chain our Interceptor service in our `services.js` file as follows:

```
.factory('myHttpInterceptor', ['$q', '$location',
  function($q, $location) {
    return {
        response: function(response) {
            return response;
        },
        responseError: function(response) {
            if (response.status === 401) {
                $location.path('/admin/login');
                return $q.reject(response);
            }
            return $q.reject(response);
        }
    };
}]);
```

The next step is to push this into `$httpProvider`.

We will add the following code to our `angcms/public/js/app.js` file:

```
.config(function ($httpProvider) {
    $httpProvider.interceptors.push('myHttpInterceptor');
});
```

To test whether our Interceptors are working or not, open up a new tab in the browser in Incognito or private browsing mode and try to directly put in the URL to edit a page; it would be something like `http://localhost:3000/admin/add-edit-page/<_id>`.

It should automatically redirect you to the login page.

Building the frontend of our CMS

All this while, we have been working on the backend and admin sections of the CMS.

Now, we will work on the frontend, the public-facing side of the website.

As the public-facing side of the website needs to have a neat layout with a logo, navigation bar, content area, footer, and so on, we are going to tweak the index page layout.

Update the `angcms/public/index.html` file with the upcoming changes.

As we would like to control some application-level settings such as the logo, footer, and so on, we first bind `AppCtrl` to the `<body>` tag, as shown in the following code:

```
<body ng-controller="AppCtrl">
```

Next, we add the following markup:

```
<div admin-login class="col-md-3 pull-right"></div>
<div class="container">
    <header>
        <img ng-src="{{site.logo}}">
    </header>
    <div message-flash></div>
    <div class="row">
        <div class="col-md-3" nav-bar></div>
        <div class="col-md-6" ng-view></div>
    </div>
    <footer>{{site.footer}}</footer>
</div>
```

As you can see from the markup, we are calling in two directives: `admin-login`, which will display a welcome message to the logged-in user, and `nav-bar`, which will show relevant navigation links on the left-hand side of the window.

We also plan to have a scope object called `site` and are displaying the site logo and site footer on this template.

The next step is to create our `AppCtrl` function in our controller, which is done as follows:

```
.controller('AppCtrl', ['$scope','AuthService',
  'flashMessageService','$location',
      function($scope,AuthService,flashMessageService,$location) {
        $scope.site = {
            logo: "img/angcms-logo.png",
            footer: "Copyright 2014 Angular CMS"
        };
    }
])
```

Refresh the page and notice the logo and footer. Needless to say, ensure that you have a logo named `angcms-logo.png` present in the `img` folder.

Building our navigation bar directive

We would like our navigation bar to display the links for all the pages created via the admin. We would like these links to be displayed in a sequence based on their `menuIndex` values.

We would also like this directive to display the admin menu links when the user is in the admin section.

With these goals in mind, let's create our directive in the `directives.js` file as follows:

```
directive('navBar', [
  function() {
    return {
      controller: function($scope, pagesFactory, $location) {
        var path = $location.path().substr(0, 6);
        if (path == "/admin") {
          $scope.navLinks = [{
            title: 'Pages',
            url: 'admin'
          }, {
```

```
                title: 'Site Settings',
                url: 'admin/site-settings'
            }, ];
        } else {
            pagesFactory.getPages().then(
                function(response) {
                    $scope.navLinks = response.data;
                }, function() {

                });
            }
        },
        templateUrl: 'partials/directives/nav.html'

    };
}
])
```

What we are doing here is using `$location.path`, we are trying to see whether the user is in the admin section or on the frontend, and based on this, we are populating the `navLinks` scope object with the relevant menu links.

Next, let's create the template for this directive. Create a new file named `nav.html` in `angcms/public/partials/directives/nav.html`, and add the following code:

```
<ul class="nav-links">
<li ng-repeat="nav in navLinks | orderBy:'menuIndex'">
    <a href="/{{nav.url}}">{{nav.title}}</a>
</li>
</ul>
```

As you see, we are using `ng-repeat` to list out our entire page menu and ordering it with the help of `menuIndex`.

Building the admin-login directive

The next directive that we'll build is the admin login, which will display the `Welcome <username>` message and have additional links to jump to the admin or log out.

Let's add the following directive to the `directives.js` file:

```
.directive('adminLogin', [
    function() {
        return {
            controller: function($scope, $cookies) {
```

```
        $scope.loggedInUser = $cookies.loggedInUser;
    },
    templateUrl: 'partials/directives/admin-login.html'
};
  }
]);
```

The controller code is straightforward, and it simply assigns the `loggedInUser` value from the cookie to the scope object.

We will create it's template as a new file in `partials/directives/admin-login.html` as follows:

```
<div ng-if=loggedInUser>
    Welcome {{loggedInUser}} |  <a href="admin/pages">My Admin
        </a> | <a href ng-click='logout()'>Logout</a>
</div>
```

Next, we will quickly write the code for the `logout` method. As this directive is within the scope of `AppCtrl`, we will write this method within the `AppCtrl` function as follows:

```
$scope.logout = function() {
  AuthService.logout().then(
    function() {

      $location.path('/admin/login');
      flashMessageService.setMessage("Successfully logged out");

    }, function(err) {
       console.log('there was an error tying to logout');
    });
};
```

Displaying the content of a page

The last and most crucial step of this entire project is to display the actual content of the selected page.

This will require us to create a new route that will accept route params. Let's get this done first in our `public/js/app.js` file as follows:

```
$routeProvider.when('/:url', {
    templateUrl: 'partials/page.html',
    controller: 'PageCtrl'
});
```

Next, let's create the partials view as a new file called `partials/page.html` with the following content:

```
<h1>{{pageContent.title}}</h1>
<div ng-bind-html="pageContent.content"></div>
```

We are using the `ng-bind-html` directive here so that the HTML content is rendered correctly instead of it spitting out the raw HTML as it is.

Next, let's create our `PageCtrl` function in `controllers.js` as follows:

```
.controller('PageCtrl',  [ '$scope','pagesFactory', '$routeParams
', function($scope, pagesFactory, $routeParams) {
  var url = $routeParams.url;
  pagesFactory.getPageContent(url).then(
    function(response) {
      $scope.pageContent = response.data;
    }, function() {
      console.log('error fetching data');
    });
}]);
```

Save the file, refresh the site, and hit any of the frontend links. You'll get an error in your console; you will see something like the following screenshot:

So, what went wrong here? What is `$sce`?

One of the coolest things about testing AngularJS apps in Google Chrome is whenever there is an error message, AngularJS has a hyperlink that will take you directly to the site that explains what the error is.

By reading up on the link, you'll get to know that the **Strict Contextual Escaping (SCE)** mode of AngularJS is turned on by default, and AngularJS feels that the HTML markup on the content of our CMS pages is unsafe. To overcome this, we will need to explicitly tell $sce to trust our content. We do this in our controller by adding the following highlighted lines to the PageCtrl function:

```
.controller('PageCtrl', ['$scope','pagesFactory',
  '$routeParams', '$sce', function($scope, pagesFactory,
    $routeParams,$sce) {
      var url = $routeParams.url;
      pagesFactory.getPageContent(url).then(
        function(response) {
          $scope.pageContent = {};
          $scope.pageContent.title = response.data.title;
          $scope.pageContent.content = $sce.trustAsHtml(
            response.data.content);

        }, function() {
          console.log('error fetching data');
      });
  }])
```

Save the file and refresh any of the page URLs. Now, you should be able to see the title and page contents with the HTML formatting.

Setting the default home page

Now, our public-facing frontend is working quite well with all the nav links, content, and so on. However, when you launch the site for the first time or hit `http://localhost:3000/`, we land up with a blank screen.

To overcome this, we will make sure that our site always has a page titled **Home**.

Then, in the page controller, we will simply add the following highlighted line, which will set the default value of the URL to home in case we don't find a URL param in the current route; we will add this to the PageCtrl function:

```
var url = $routeParams.url;
if(!url) url="home";
```

Now, the home page will load by default for the preceding URL link. Alternatively, you can also set the $routeProvider redirect in the public/js/app.js file to, say, the following:

```
$routeProvider.otherwise({redirectTo: '/home'});
```

Summary

This brings us to the end of this rather long chapter.

We went full stack, right from coding our backend by building REST APIs to saving and reading data from the database. We also built the AngularJS frontend that interacts with these backend APIs.

The key takeaways from this chapter are as follows:

- Building backend web services using Node.js, MongoDB, and ExpressJS
- Securing API using sessions
- Making AngularJS and ExpressJS work together and build routes that span across both the systems
- Authenticating on the client side using Interceptors
- Integrating third-party modules
- Using custom filters to format and store data
- Building a custom module for a global notification system

In the next chapter, we will see how to deploy our Angular JS app on a cloud server and look at interesting ways in which just pure client-side apps can be deployed on the cloud.

8
Scalable Architecture for Deployments on AWS

As we enter into this chapter, we have covered nearly all aspects of building an AngularJS app and also the necessary backend that is needed to interact with our app. This chapter will focus on interesting ways of deploying our application, and how we can take advantage of the Cloud to build scalability.

Amazon Web Services, commonly known as AWS, is one of the leading and most popular Cloud platforms to deploy web applications.

What makes AWS unique is their exhaustive set of services that one can utilize to make an application truly scalable and load faster.

It would thus make sense for us to start by understanding some the popular services that AWS provides.

Understanding the various services in Amazon AWS

AWS comes with a full gamut of services that cover the various aspects useful to build a web application. In this chapter, we will cover some of the most popular ones and ones that would be of use when deploying an AngularJS app; they are as follows:

- **Amazon Elastic Compute Cloud (EC2)**: EC2 is Amazon's computing service. It allows you to select a combination of CPU power and RAM, and build a web server needed to run your web application.

- **Amazon Simple Storage Service (S3)**: The Simple Storage Service is primarily used to store a wide variety of files, mainly static files such as media files, CSS, JS, images, and so on. One can create an S3 bucket and have multiples files and folders within the bucket.

- **Amazon CloudFront**: CloudFront is Amazon's Content Delivery Network (CDN). In most cases, it is linked to an S3 bucket, and the static files from the S3 bucket are delivered via CloudFront.

- **Amazon Relational Database Service (RDS)**: RDS is a ready-to-use relational database in the Cloud. It provides a simple set of web services that allow you to manage your MySQL instance on the Cloud.

- **Amazon DynamoDB**: DynamoDB is Amazon's fully-managed NoSQL database. It is a ready-to-use database service that can easily scale.

- **Amazon Simple Email Service (SES)**: The SES is used to send out e-mail notifications from your application.

Delving into AWS deployment architectures

When deploying applications on AWS, there are numerous ways of deploying the app. One can make use of the services that AWS provides to build an architecture that can maximize performance and reduce costs. We will explore two topologies that can be used to deploy our AngularJS apps in the following sections.

The EC2 server-based architecture

The most common deployment architecture for regular web applications would be as follows:

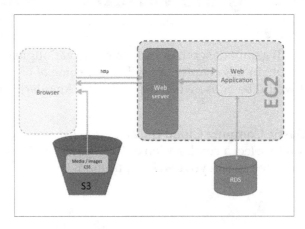

This architecture consists of an EC2 instance, which has the web server running and the application deployed on it.

It will talk to an RDS database to read and write from it. All the static files such as images, CSS, JS, and media files, if any, would be stored in an S3 bucket and directly served to the user's browser from the S3 bucket or through CloudFront.

This is a common architecture to deploy server-side apps that are built on, say, **Ruby on Rails (RoR)**, PHP, or Java. All requests are sent to the server, which dynamically generates the HTML page by pulling data from the database and placing it into content templates, and sends back the final HTML page to the browser. As you can see, the web server is doing quite a bit of heavy lifting here, and as the number of concurrent users increases, the load on the web server increases proportionately.

In such cases, the logical ways of scaling would be to bump up the commuting power of the EC2 instance, and add multiple EC2 instances under a load balancer. One would make use of AWS's **CloudWatch** and autoscaling to carry out the scaling.

The Server-less Architecture

The following topology is another alternate deployment topology on which we can deploy our app. We can make use of and look up to this topology especially to deploy pure client-side apps and in cases where data is static.

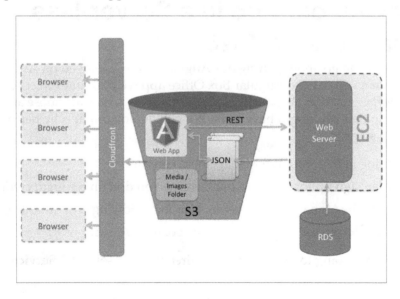

This architecture is often referred to as the **Server-less Architecture**, primarily because in this topology, the web server is sparingly used, or it can even be fully negated at times.

Here, instead of deploying our app on the EC2 instance, we would deploy it in the S3 bucket along with the images and media files. The JSON data that our AngularJS app will read from could also be cached and stored in the S3 bucket.

In this scenario, when the user visits the application for the first time, the app along with the JSON file would get downloaded to the user's browser, and after that, all the interaction would happen within the browser and the S3 bucket, thus leaving the web server free to handle only critical server-level tasks such as authentication, validation, and so on. We can also make use of CloudFront and have the S3 contents served via CloudFront; this will make our app *infinitely scalable* as now the CloudFront and S3 become the main points for serving the content. As the traffic increases, it would be divided among the numerous CloudFront nodes. A significant advantage here is that we no longer have a single point of failure for our app. In case one or more of the CloudFront nodes fail, CloudFront would automatically redirect the users to the other available node. Besides these advantages of high scalability and high availability, this architecture also has a very low hosting cost compared to running traditional EC2 instances.

Deploying our app in a Server-less Architecture on AWS

Let's look at how to go about getting our AngularJS app deployed on AWS. For this exercise, we will use the Angular Box Office app we built in *Chapter 4, Using REST Web Services in Your AngularJS App*. Alternatively, you can choose any AngularJS app that you might have built. We will deploy our app by performing the following steps:

1. First, log in to your AWS Management console.
2. You can sign up for a free account in case you don't have login credentials.
3. To go to the Management console, visit the following URL after logging in:

   `https://console.aws.amazon.com/console/home`.

4. As we are going to upload our app directly to S3, select **S3 Service**.

5. Then, click on the **Create Bucket** button and give your bucket a name; you can call it `<my-domain-name.com>`. Remember that the bucket names need to be unique across the S3 universe. Moreover, if you are planning to map a domain name to your S3 bucket, then you need to ensure that the bucket name and the domain names are the same.

6. The next step is to let S3 know that we will be using it to host our website. For this, we select our S3 bucket, and then in the **Properties** section, on the right-hand side, we select the accordion called **Static Website Hosting**.

7. We then select the radio button called **Enable website hosting**, and enter the names of our home page and custom error pages.

8. Also, note down the URL of the end point as this is where our app will be hosted. The following screenshot shows the **Static Website Hosting** window:

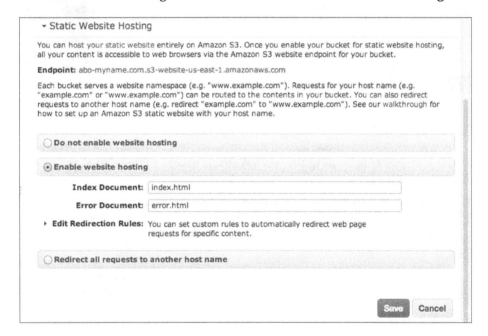

9. Once this is done, the next step is to upload our files. Under the **Actions** menu, select **Upload**, and the **Upload – Select Files and Folders** window pops up, as shown in the following screenshot:

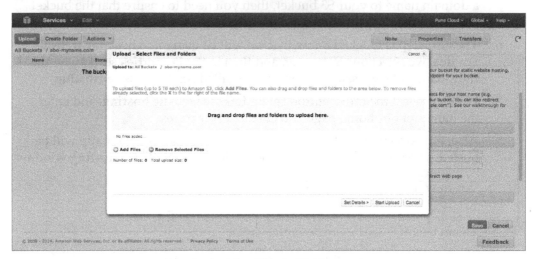

The **Upload – Select Files and Folders** window

10. Use the enhanced uploader or the drag-and-drop feature to upload multiple files at once. Once these files are uploaded, they will still not be visible to the end users, as by default, AWS restricts access to these files only to the logged-in user.

11. The last step is to make our files public. We do this by selecting the checkbox against all these files and folders, right-clicking on them, and selecting the **Make Public** menu item. This is shown in the following screenshot:

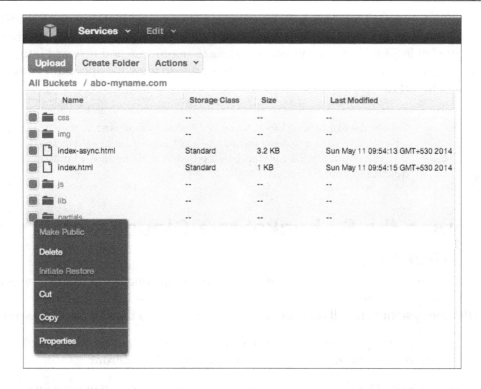

12. You can also attach a bucket policy to automatically make all the items in the bucket public.

13. Hit the S3 Endpoint URL in the browser, and your app should load on the browser.

Mapping a domain to S3

In case you have your app served out of S3, you would want to map your domain to the S3 bucket. Mapping a domain to an S3 bucket is rather straightforward; we need to perform the following steps:

1. Make sure your bucket name is the same as that of your domain name.

2. Map the value of **CNAMEs** to `s3.amazonaws.com`.

3. Wait for the DNS servers to update themselves and you should be set.

This will now map `http://my-domain-name.com` to our app that runs from the S3 bucket. However, to map `www.my-domain-name.com`, you'll need to create another empty bucket in S3 with the name `www.my-domain-name.com` and forward it to `http://my-domain-name.com` so that the user is able to view the app, both with www and without it.

 Follow the guide on AWS at `http://docs.aws.amazon.com/AmazonS3/latest/dev/website-hosting-custom-domain-walkthrough.html` for step-by-step instructions on how to map a domain to your S3 bucket.

Mapping the S3 bucket to a CloudFront distribution

The S3 by itself can handle a reasonably large number of concurrent users. However, to further improve concurrency and response time, we can add a CloudFront distribution system that will replicate the S3 contents across the various edge servers.

Adding a CloudFront distribution is rather easy. From the Management console, navigate to **Services** | **Storage and Content Delivery** | **CloudFront**.

Click on the **Create Distribution** button and select the S3 bucket name we just created. Set the rest of the parameters according to your preference and save it. Wait for a few hours for the content to replicate across the servers.

Once the replication is complete, hit the CloudFront URL in the browser and see your app working.

Getting your app ready for production deployment

What we just uploaded to S3 was fully functional, but it wasn't quite production-ready from a performance standpoint. If you ran it through the YSlow Firebug add-on or Google Page Speed, you'll notice it doesn't get a very high performance score. You'll probably get a "C" grade on YSlow.

Improving the page-load time of your app

Currently, our app has about seven external JavaScript files, two CSS files, and some custom web fonts included in it. These are about nine additional HTTP requests that need to be made before the full content can be displayed.

Ideally, for production deployments, our JavaScript files need to be concatenated and minified. We will do this by using Grunt, an excellent Node- and JavaScript-based task runner. You can alternatively look at either **gulp.js** (www.gulpjs.com) or **Brunch** (www.brunch.io), which are similar build tools that claim to be fast and also have some interesting plugins you can make use of.

If you have completed *Chapter 2, Setting Up Your Rig*, you should already be running grunt-cli, the command-line version of Grunt.

If not, then let's first install grunt cli using the following command line:

```
npm install -g grunt-cli
```

We install grunt-cli globally as we are going to need it across multiple projects.

Once grunt-cli is installed, the next step is to install Grunt and its other dev-dependencies. We do this by updating the package.json file location in the root of our abo folder using the following highlighted code:

```
{
    "name": "abo",
    "description": "Angular Box Office",
    "devDependencies": {
        . . .
        "grunt": "~0.4.2",
        "grunt-contrib-concat": "~0.4.0",
        "grunt-contrib-uglify": "~0.2.2"

    }
}
```

For this exercise, we will concatenate and minify our JS files, and hence, along with Grunt, we will install grunt-contrib-concat and grunt-contrib-uglify.

The next step is to install these node modules using the following terminal command:

```
npm install
```

Once they are installed, we will start with writing our Grunt tasks. We will first create our `Gruntfile.js` file in the root of the `abo` folder, and start by writing our wrapper function, initializing our configuration object, and reading the project setting from our `package.json` file as follows:

```
module.exports = function(grunt) {
    grunt.initConfig({
        pkg: grunt.file.readJSON('package.json'),
    });
};
```

Next, we start writing our Grunt tasks within our `grunt.initConfig` method. The first task is to concatenate our JS file; the code for this is as follows:

```
concat: {
    options: {
        //define a string to put between each file in the
        //concatenated output
        separator: ';'
    },
    dist: {
        // the files to concatenate
        src: ['app/bower_components/angular/angular.js',
'app/bower_components/angular-route/angular-route.js',
            'app/js/**/*.js'],
        // the location of the resulting JS file
        dest: 'app/build/<%= pkg.name %>.js'
    }
}
```

Here, under the `concat` task, we define the separator used between the two files that are concatenated. Then, we provide the source list of files that we would like to concatenate. For this exercise, say we would like to concatenate the `angular.js` and `angular-route.js` files from our `lib` folder and all the files in our `js` folder. We take advantage of wild cards instead of having to mention each and every file within the `js` folder.

At times, you may choose not to concatenate the library files such as `angular.js` and `angular-route.js`, but instead, you may call them from a CDN. The decision is based on trying to strike the right balance between the file size of the concatenated file and the number of HTTP requests to load the nonconcatenated files. Another advantage of loading the files from a CDN such as Google is that there is a good chance the library files could have already been cached on the user's browser cache and will not be downloaded again.

The next section is the destination where you'd like to save the concatenated file. In case the folder isn't present, then Grunt will autocreate that folder. We can also use variable names such as `pkg.name` to set a new name for the concatenated JS file.

The second task, which we will create, is to minify the concatenated JS file. We do this with the following piece of code:

```
uglify: {
  options: {
    banner: '/*! <%= pkg.name %> <%=
      grunt.template.today("yyyy-mm-dd") %> */\n'
  },
  build: {
    src: 'app/build/<%= pkg.name %>.js',
    dest: 'app/build/<%= pkg.name %>.min.js'
  }
}
```

Ensure you separate each task with a comma. The banner is optional and it would merely add a comment line at the top of the file stating the date it was created.

The `src` and `dest` options under `build` should be self-explanatory now. We take our concatenated file and minify it and save it with the `.min.js` extension in the same `build` folder.

The next step is to load the plugins that perform these tasks. This is done by using the following code:

```
grunt.loadNpmTasks('grunt-contrib-concat');
grunt.loadNpmTasks('grunt-contrib-uglify');
```

Finally, we will register our default task using the following code:

```
grunt.registerTask('default', ['concat','uglify']);
```

You can choose to register different tasks. For example, you can have an additional task that runs, say JSHint, depending on the activities you'd want to do.

Verify whether your final Grunt file looks something like the following:

```
module.exports = function(grunt) {
    // Project configuration.
    grunt.initConfig({
        pkg: grunt.file.readJSON('package.json'),
        concat: {
            options: {
                // define a string to put between each file in the
                // concatenated output
                separator: ';'
            },
            dist: {
                // the files to concatenate
                src: ['app/bower_components/angular/angular.js',
                    'app/bower_components/angular-route/angular-route.
                    js',
                        'app/js/**/*.js'],
                // the location of the resulting JS file
                dest: 'app/build/<%= pkg.name %>.js'
            }
        },
        uglify: {
            options: {
                banner: '/*! <%= pkg.name %> <%=
                    grunt.template.today("yyyy-mm-dd") %> */\n'
            },
            build: {
                src: 'app/build/<%= pkg.name %>.js',
                dest: 'app/build/<%= pkg.name %>.min.js'
            }
        },
    })
    // Load the plugin that provides the "uglify" task.
    grunt.loadNpmTasks('grunt-contrib-concat');
    grunt.loadNpmTasks('grunt-contrib-uglify');
    // Default task(s).
    grunt.registerTask('default', ['concat', 'uglify']);

};
```

Save the file, and in the terminal, run the following command:

```
grunt
```

This should create the `build` folder, and put in the concatenated and minified version of the file as `abo.min.js`.

It is important to note that while minifying AngularJS files, `uglify` will replace function arguments with single characters. This will obviously create problems for us since we use these function arguments to pass our dependencies, and with the replaced names, the dependency injector will not be able to identify the dependencies.

To overcome this, make sure to use inline notation when defining the dependency injection. For example, we should be using the following code:

```
controller('MovieListCtrl', ['$scope','$rtmFactory',
    function($scope,$rtmFactory) {
```

The last step is to replace the linking of those multiple JS files with our new concatenated and minified JS file in the `index.html` file.

 One can also look at the excellent plugin called `ngmin` (`https://github.com/btford/ngmin`) by Brian Ford, which will help change them to inline notation.

Reupload the `index.html` file along with the new `abo.min.js` file and ensure you have set them to **Make Public**.

Setting Expires headers

A recommended best practice is to set Expires headers for static files that aren't going to change often. In our case, we should ideally set Expires headers for the following items:

- `index.html`
- `abo.min.js`
- `app.css`

We do this by selecting each of these items in the AWS Management console, and in the **Properties** section, select the **Metadata** accordion, and add the following keys:

- `Cache-Control` with a very high value
- `Expires` with a value of a futuristic date

The output of the preceding keys is shown in the following screenshot:

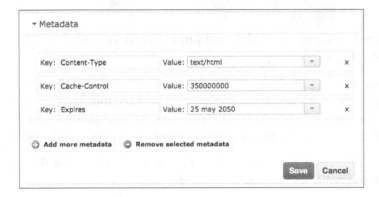

Repeat the same for the other resource items mentioned in the section.

 Ideally, we would append a version number or a timestamp to our JS and CSS files so that when a new file with a different filename is uploaded, it will force-download the latest file instead of taking it from the user's browser cache.

Performance

Our app is now deployed in the production mode. If you try and run YSlow on this new updated version, you should get an "A" Grade now, as shown in the following screenshot:

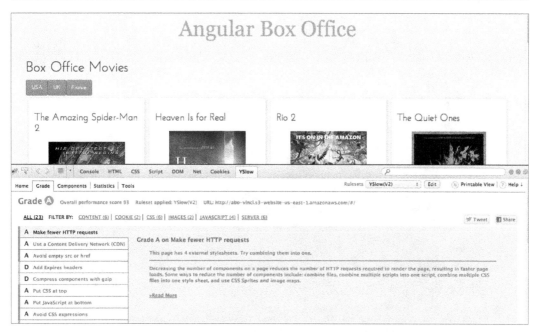

The **Angular Box Office** window displaying the Grade

Carrying out the other recommendations made by YSlow can always further increase the performance score, but we will stop here for now.

Summary

In this chapter, we saw the different architectures in which an AngularJS app can be deployed on AWS Cloud.

We went through the details of deploying our app in a Server-less Architecture by making use of S3 and CloudFront. Finally, we saw how to get our app ready for production by concatenating and minifying our JS files and ensuring our app gets a high performance score.

While AWS's services have been available for production use for a long time, we can deploy our AngularJS app in a similar architecture on Rackspace Cloud files, Google App Engine, or even GitHub pages. Do explore these options and see which of them give you the best results in terms of performance and ease of use.

9
Building an E-Commerce Store

In this chapter, we are going to build an eBay-style e-commerce store that we will call Garage Commerce. It will be a store where users can upload and list items they would usually put up for a Garage Sale. Authenticated users can browse through the products and buy them.

Some of the interesting topics that we will cover are as follows:

- Using AWS DynamoDB and S3 to store our product information
- Using Facebook login and AWS's Web Identity Federation to authenticate users
- Using the UI-Router to build nested views

As one would know, building an e-commerce store requires some heavy backend coding and extensive interactions with a database. A couple of years back, the thought of building an e-commerce store using just client-side scripts would have sounded quite absurd. However, thanks to a new breed of BaaS services, it is now possible to build a full-fledged e-commerce store just using JavaScript.

Backend as a Service

Backend as a Service (**BaaS**), sometimes also referred to as **Mobile Backend as a Service** (**MBaaS**), is quickly gaining popularity as it helps application developers to quickly build client-side or mobile applications without having to worry about the database or server-side part of the application.

Some of the popular BaaS services are as follows:

- Parse (`https://parse.com/`)
- Firebase (`https://www.firebase.com/`)
- Kinvey (`http://www.kinvey.com/`)
- AWS (`http://aws.amazon.com/`)

Besides providing APIs to perform CRUD and query operations on a database, most of these BaaS offer additional benefits such as easier OAuth sign on using Facebook and Google.

Firebase is a nice tool that automatically syncs data across all connected devices. AngularFire is a helper library that makes it easy to integrate Firebase with AngularJS.

While AWS does not project itself as a BaaS provider, one can make use of a combination of its various services to work like a BaaS.

Building a BaaS platform on AWS

For this particular chapter, we will choose to use AWS to build our backed service. Amazon has lately released a JavaScript-based SDK called the AWS JS SDK that allows us to connect and work with the various AWS services using plain, simple JavaScript.

You can read more about the JS SDK and download it from `https://aws.amazon.com/sdkforbrowser/`.

We will be making use of the following AWS services to build our backend:

- **DynamoDB**: This is Amazon's fully managed and highly scalable NoSQL database.
- **Simple Storage Service (S3)**: This is used to store images, CSS, and other types of static files. You will remember using this S3 service in *Chapter 8, Scalable Architecture for Deployments on AWS*.
- **AWS Identity and Access Management (IAM)**: This is a core service that allows us to create user groups, roles, and define access rights to the various AWS services for the created roles.
- **AWS Security Token Service (STS)**: The security token service goes hand in hand with the IAM service. As the name suggests, this services provides temporary, limited privilege credentials to the IAM or Federated Users user.

- **Web Identity Federation (WIF)**: This is a new feature within the STS. It allows us to use authenticated access tokens from third-party identity providers such as Facebook, Google, or Amazon to allow access to the AWS services.

Setting up an S3 Bucket with public read access

In the previous chapter, we saw how to create an S3 bucket on AWS and upload files using their online dashboard. We also saw how to give it public read access so that they would be visible to everybody on the Internet.

In our case, as the images are going to be uploaded via the end users, we will need to set bucket level policies so that all the uploaded images automatically become public.

Let's now see how to go about doing it:

1. First, log in to the **AWS Management Console** at `https://console.aws.amazon.com/console/home`. Navigate to the S3 service and create a bucket name. I'm calling mine `garage-commerce`. Preferably select `us-east-1` as a region so as to easily follow the steps in this chapter.

2. Go to the **Properties** panel and select **Permissions Accordion**, click on the **Add bucket policy** button, and add the following bucket policy in the pop up that comes up:

```
{
    "Version": "2008-10-17",
    "Statement": [
        {
            "Sid": "AllowPublicRead",
            "Effect": "Allow",
            "Principal": {
                "AWS": "*"
            },
            "Action": "s3:GetObject",
            "Resource": "arn:aws:s3:::garage-commerce/*"
        }
    ]
}
```

 Make sure that you replace the `garage-commerce` word in the last line with the name of your bucket.

3. Save the policy and close it.

Setting up the CORS policy on your S3 bucket

Cross-origin resource sharing (CORS) is a way to allow applications hosted on one domain to interact with resources on another domain.

By default, AWS allows only GET methods for all domains, as we need to be able to read and write to the S3 bucket form our localhost application, we need to add a custom CORS rule.

To add the custom rule, click on the **Add CORS configuration** button within the permissions accordion, and add the following CORS policy to allow localhost to write to S3:

```xml
<?xml version="1.0" encoding="UTF-8"?>
<CORSConfiguration xmlns="http://s3.amazonaws.com/doc/2006-03-01/">
    <CORSRule>
        <AllowedOrigin>http://localhost:8000</AllowedOrigin>
        <AllowedMethod>HEAD</AllowedMethod>
        <AllowedMethod>GET</AllowedMethod>
        <AllowedMethod>PUT</AllowedMethod>
        <AllowedMethod>POST</AllowedMethod>
        <AllowedMethod>DELETE</AllowedMethod>
        <AllowedHeader>*</AllowedHeader>
    </CORSRule>
</CORSConfiguration>
```

Creating our DynamoDB tables

Next, we will create our DynamoDB table. So, from the **Management Console** or the **Services** drop-down link, head to the DynamoDB service and follow these steps. For the sake of consistency, select the US East (N. Virginia) region:

1. Click on the **Create Table** button and call it `garage-commerce`. Set the **Primary Key** type to **Hash**, and set the **Hash Attribute Name** as `product_id`, as shown in the following screenshot. Then, click on the **Continue** button:

2. We will leave the **Add Indexes** screen as it is and continue to the next step.

3. On the **Provisioned Throughput Capacity Section**, we will set the following:

   ° **Read Capacity Units**: 10

   ° **Write Capacity Units**: 5

> The capacity unit defines the number of requests that come in every second. The values 10 for read and 5 for write are the limits of the free tier and are sufficient during the development phase. During production, this value can be throttled up as required.

4. On the next **Throughput Alarm Option**, you can choose to give an e-mail address to receive notifications or leave it blank.

5. Review the details on the next **Summary Page** and click on the **Create Button**.

Your table should now be visible in the DynamoDB control panel.

Creating the Identity and Access Management (IAM) role

Let's now head over to the IAM link from the AWS management console or the services link:

1. In IAM, go to the **Roles** section from the navigation screen on the left-hand side, and create a new role.

2. Create a user called `garageCommerceUser`.

3. On the **Configure Role** screen, select the **Role for Identity Provider Access** radio button.

4. Select the **Grant access to web identity providers** button.

5. On the next screen, select **Facebook** as the **Identity Provider**, and enter the application ID of the Facebook app you created on Facebook.

6. On the next **Establish Trust** screen, review the default policy created by AWS and click on **Continue**.

7. On the next **Set Permissions** screen, select the **No Permissions** radio button and create the rule.

8. Once the User shows up in the list of **User Roles**, select **garageCommerceUser**. On the **Permissions** tab, click on the **Attach role policy** button and select **Power User Access**, as shown in the following screenshot:

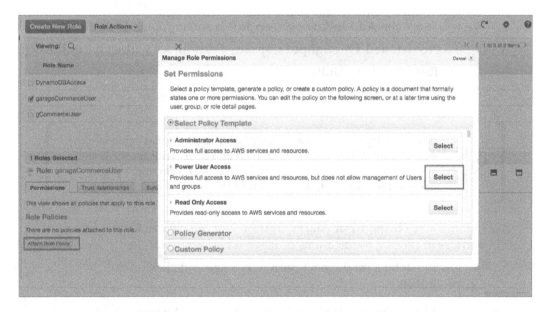

This should allow our user role to have the necessary permissions to interact with the S3 and DynamoDB services.

Creating our e-commerce app

Now that we have everything set up on the AWS side, let's start by building our AngularJS app.

As always, we will start by downloading the forked AngularJS Seed project from GitHub at `https://github.com/areai51/angular-seed` and getting it set up.

Before we run the npm install command, let's add a few more dependencies to our `bower.json` file to install `angular-animate` and `angular-ui-router`, as we are going to use these in our project.

Please modify your `bower.json` file as highlighted:

```
{
  "name": "angular-seed",
  "description": "A starter project for AngularJS",
  "version": "0.0.0",
  "homepage": "https://github.com/angular/angular-seed",
  "license": "MIT",
  "private": true,
  "dependencies": {
    "angular": "1.2.x",
    "angular-ui-router": "0.2.10",
    "angular-animate": "1.2.x",
    "angular-facebook": "",
    "angular-loader": "1.2.x",
    "angular-mocks": "~1.2.x",
    "html5-boilerplate": "~4.3.0"
  }
}
```

Alternatively, you could simply run the following command in the terminal:

bower install –save angular-ui-router angular-animate angular-facebook

This will automatically add the entries to the `bower.json` file.

Save the file, and run the npm install command in the terminal. Next, run the npm start command; this will install the bower components and start the web server on port 8000.

You should have the site running from http://localhost:8000/app.

Building nested views using UI-Router

From all the various examples so far, we have been using ngRoute and ng-view to render our pages. It has worked fine so far because in all these cases, each of our pages was different from the other, and the entire view would change from one route URL to another.

However, when building large complex applications, we will come across scenarios where we need to create nested views and update only a certain section of the view, based on the user's interaction.

The UI-Router, https://github.com/angular-ui/ui-router, allows us to build such nested views. Unlike the route provider, where the mapping is based on URL routes, with the UI-Router, the interface is organized as states. Let's see how to go about using the UI-Router in our application.

Let's start by modifying our index.html file as highlighted:

```
<body>
  <ul class="menu">
    <li><a href="#/toys">Toys</a></li>
    <li><a href="#/books">Books</a></li>
  </ul>

  <!--[if lt IE 7]>
      <p class="browsehappy">You are using an <strong>outdated</
strong> browser. Please <a href="http://browsehappy.com/">upgrade your
browser</a> to improve your experience.</p>
  <![endif]-->

  <div ui-view></div>


  <!-- In production use:
  <script src="//ajax.googleapis.com/ajax/libs/angularjs/x.x.x/
angular.min.js"></script>
  -->
  <script src="bower_components/angular/angular.js"></script>
```

```
    <script src="bower_components/angular-ui-router/release/angular-ui-
router.js"></script>
    <script src="js/app.js"></script>
    <script src="js/services.js"></script>
    <script src="js/controllers.js"></script>
    <script src="js/filters.js"></script>
    <script src="js/directives.js"></script>
</body>
```

The first thing we do is include our `angular-ui-router.js` file. Next, as `ui-router` uses the `ui-view` directive, we replace `ng-view` with `ui-view`.

Finally, just so that we can test our nested views, we'll add two dummy category links called `Toys` and `Books`.

We will also need to inject `ui-route` into our app as a dependency. We do this in the `app.js` file as highlighted:

```
angular.module('myApp', [
    'ui.router',
    'myApp.filters',
    'myApp.services',
    'myApp.directives',
    'myApp.controllers'
])
```

Make sure you remove `ngRoute` that comes in as a part of the boilerplate.

Mapping states to URL, views, and controllers

As the UI-Router works around states, we'll need to map states to the corresponding URL, views, and controllers. We'll do this in our `app.js` file as follows:

```
config(['$stateProvider',
    function($stateProvider) {
        $stateProvider.state('add', {
          url:'/add',
            templateUrl: 'partials/add-products.html',
            controller: 'AddProductsCtrl'
        });
        $stateProvider.state('category', {
          url:'/:category',
            templateUrl: 'partials/products.html',
            controller: 'ProductsCtrl'
        });
```

```
                $stateProvider.state('category.products', {
                url:'/:id',
                  templateUrl: 'partials/products.details.html',
                  controller: 'ProductDetailsCtrl'
                });
        }
    ])
```

The first state that we define is to add products; it is mapped to the `add-products.html` partial and the `AddProductsCtrl` controller. We then define the category state and use a variable to define the category, which will be mapped to the `products.html` view and the `ProductsCtrl` controller.

The next state is a nested view where we define the product state as a subset of the category, using the dot notation. The URL is a variable called ID, which would essentially be the product ID. We again make use of the dot notation to define the partial for the `products.details.html` view.

Prototyping our application

Many a times, while building large client-side applications, things get a lot clearer when we start with designing our layout and views and, in general, setting up the application click flow.

We will start by using bootstrap to get our basic grid in place.

Setting up our index.html file

Let's open up our `index.html` file and add the Bootstrap CSS. For the sake of convenience, we will use the Simplex Bootswatch theme by adding its CDN link as follows:

```
<link rel="stylesheet" href="//netdna.bootstrapcdn.com/
bootswatch/3.1.1/simplex/bootstrap.min.css"/>
```

Next, we will add the navigation bar just under the body tag or our `index.html` file, as shown in the following code:

```
        <nav class="navbar navbar-fixed navbar-inverse" role="navigation">
        <div class="container">
          <a class="navbar-brand" href="/">Garage Commerce</a>
            <ul class="nav navbar-nav">
        <li><a href="#/toys">Toys</a></li>
        <li><a href="#/books">Books</a></li>
      </ul>
      </nav>
```

Next, we will add the `container-fluid` class to our `ui-view` as follows:

```html
<div class="container-fluid">
<div  ui-view></div>
</div>
```

Creating the controllers

Let's open up the `js/controllers.js` file, and add the controller functions with
some dummy scope data:

```javascript
'use strict';
angular.module('myApp.controllers', []).controller('ProductsCtrl',
['$scope', '$stateParams',
        function($scope, $stateParams) {
            $scope.category = $stateParams.category
            $scope.productsListing = [{
                    product_id: '123',
                    title: ' Baby Rattles',
                    price: 2,
                    userName: 'John Doe'
                }, {
                    product_id: '456',
                    title: ' Kiddy Laptop',
                    price: 12,
                    userName: 'Sandy Peters'
                }

            ]

        }
    ])
    .controller('ProductDetailsCtrl', ['$scope',
'$stateParams',function($scope, $stateParams) {
            $scope.id = $stateParams.id;
            $scope.product = {
                'title': 'Kiddy Laptop',
                'description': 'lorem lipsum do re me.',
                'price': 12,
                'userName': 'Sandy Peters'

            }

        }
    ]);
```

Essentially, what we are doing here is injecting the `stateParams` object and storing the category and ID values into scope objects.

We are also setting up the `$products` scope objects with dummy data.

Creating the product partials

With the controllers in place, let's work on getting our partials ready.

Create a new file called `products.html` in the `partials` folder. This will be our product listing page. Let's add the following code:

```
<h1>{{category}}</h1>
<hr/>
<!-- 1st Column -->
<div class="col-md-5">
    <div class="row-fluid listing sidebar" >
    <div class="listing" ng-repeat="product in productsListing">

    <h2><a ng-href="#/{{category
      +'/'+product.product_id}}">{{product.title}}</a> </h2>

    <h5>{{product.price |currency}}</h5>

    <p><i>-by:{{product.userName}}</i></p>
    </div>
    </div>

</div>
</div>

<!-- 2nd Column -->
<div class="col-md-7">
    <div class="slide" ui-view></div>
</div>
```

We are splitting our product listing page layout into two columns. On the left column, we will be listing out our products, and on the right column, we will display the details of the selected product.

As you might have noticed, the right-hand column has a nested view within which we plan to show our product details. From a usability point of view, this kind of a layout would allow users to quickly browse through products, without having to toggle back and forth between the product listing and details page, as it would have been the case in traditional e-commerce sites.

Let's create our product details page within the `partials` folder; we will call the page `products.details.html`. We use the dot notation to define the parent and child state views. In our case, the product is the parent to the details view.

It is important to follow the right dot notations and naming conventions to ensure that the UI-Router is able to properly load the nested views. Add the following code to the `products.details.html` page:

```
<p class="title">{{id}}</p>
<h1>{{product.title}}</h1>
<p>{{product.description}}</p>
<h3>{{product.price|currency}}</h3>
```

Save the files, refresh the app in the browser, and click on the category and product links to ensure that all the views are loading up properly.

Adding animations to the view transitions

The beauty of single-page apps is that they allow you to add interesting transition effects and animations. In this case, we would like our product details view to slide in from the right, each time a product is selected from the listing.

We will do this using the `ngAnimate` module. The first step is to include our `angular-animate` js library in the `index.html` file as follows:

```
<script src="bower_components/angular-animate/angular-animate.js">
  </script>
```

Next, we include `ngAnimate` as a dependency for our app in the `app.js` file as follows:

```
angular.module('myApp', [
  ..........
  'ngAnimate'
])
```

Adding in the CSS transition effects

The `ngAnimate` module works in a slightly different way with the UI-Router as compared to `ngRoute`. In the case of `ngRoute`, the animation classes such as `ng-enter`, `ng-leave`, and `ng-enter-active` are automatically added.

In the case of the UI-Router, we need to define a CSS class called `slide`, and the `ng-enter` and `ng-leave` classes are linked to it. This is why we added the slide CSS class to the `ui-view` div on the second column of the product-listing partial.

Let's now add the CSS transition effects in our `app.css` file as follows:

```css
.slide {
    -webkit-transition: 0.5s ease-in-out all;
    transition: 0.5s ease-in-out all;
    position: relative;
}

.slide.ng-enter {
    position: absolute;
    left: 100% ;
}

.slide.ng-enter.ng-enter-active {
    left: 10%
}
```

What we are doing here is we are setting the transition time and easing effect on the main slide class.

Then, we create our `ng-enter` class, which is the starting position of the animation, and the `ng-enter-active` class, which is the ending position of our animation.

Save the file, and test the application on the browser. As you select a product, you'll notice it entering the screen; however, you'll also notice that due to the previous product staying in place, there is a bit of a jump in the animation. We need to gracefully fade out the previous product while the new product is entering in. We do this by adding the `ng-leave` and `ng-leave-active` CSS classes as follows:

```css
.slide.ng-leave {
    opacity: 0.5
}

.slide.ng-leave.ng-leave-active {
    opacity: 0;
}
```

Test your application, and things should be looking good. This is how we are aiming for our final application to work.

Creating our application-level controller

As we build our app, we are going to need a couple of scope objects that would be used across the entire application.

We can define these objects in an `AppCtrl` controller and map it high up in the DOM tree structure so that they can be easily inherited down to the child scopes. Create the `AppCtrl` controller function in our `controllers.js` file and then add the following scope objects:

```
.controller('AppCtrl', ['$scope', 'categoryService',
        function($scope, categoryService) {
            $scope.categories = categoryService.getCategories();
            $scope.user = {};
            $scope.shoppingBasket = [ ];
        }
]);
```

As you can see, we are making use of both `getCategories` and `categoryService`. So, let's go ahead and create these in our `services.js` file as follows:

```
.factory("categoryService", [function() {
        return {

            getCategories: function() {
                var categories = ['Toys', 'Electronics', 'Books',
                    'Furniture', 'Collectibles'];
                return categories;
            }
        }

    }
]);
```

Now, let's attach the `AppCtrl` controller to the body element in our `index.html` file, as shown in the following code:

```
<body ng-controller='AppCtrl'>
```

While we are at it, let's also replace our static navigation menu with the dynamic one:

```
<ul class="nav navbar-nav">
    <li ng-repeat="category in categories"> <a href="#/
{{category}}">{{category}}</a>
    </li>
</ul>
```

Adding a Facebook login

Now that we know how our application would work, we'll start making it functional. As we are using Facebook as our identity provider, and also as we plan to have our users log in via Facebook to be able to add their products and make purchases, we will need to integrate Facebook with our app.

There are quite a few Facebook modules available for Angular JS. We will be using the module called `angular-facebook`, which is available at `https://github.com/Ciul/angular-facebook`.

If you recollect, we added this as a dependency in our `bower.json` file, and it is already downloaded along with our other libraries.

Let's include this library into our `index.html` file as follows:

```
<script src="bower_components/angular-facebook/lib/angular-facebook.js"></script>
```

The next step is to include it as a dependency in our `app.js` file:

```
angular.module('myApp', [
  ......
  'facebook'
])
```

We also need to define our Facebook app ID as a `config` parameter; we do this in the same `app.js` file as follows:

```
.config(['FacebookProvider',function(FacebookProvider){
    FacebookProvider.init('<facebook app id>');
}])
```

We will now create our factory service that will contain functions to log in and return the user details of the person who has already logged in. Create the `authService` factory function within the `services.js` file as follows:

```
.factory('authService', ['$q', 'Facebook',
    function($q, Facebook) {
        return {

getUserInfo: function() {
                var d = $q.defer();
                Facebook.api('/me', function(response) {
                    d.resolve(response);
                });
                return d.promise;
```

```
            },
        };
    }
]);
```

While creating our `authService` function, we inject `$q` and `Facebook` as dependencies. The `getUserInfo` method wraps the `FacebookAPI` request for the `/me` endpoint and returns the logged in user's data object. Notice that we are making use of `promise` to ensure that we get a response with the data.

Next, we will add functionality to our `AppCtrl` controller to check if the user is logged in and has authorized our app. Add the highlighted code as follows:

```
.controller('AppCtrl', ['$scope', 'categoryService', 'Facebook',
'authService',
    function($scope, categoryService, Facebook, authService) {
        $scope.categories = categoryService.getCategories();
        $scope.user = {}
        $scope.shoppingBasket = [ ];
        Facebook.getLoginStatus(function(response) {


            if (response.status === 'connected') {
                authService.getUserInfo().then(function(data) {
                    $scope.user = data;
                });
            } else {
                Facebook.login();
            };

        });


    }
])
```

We first call the `getLoginStatus` method and check if the response status is connected, that is, we check whether the user has logged in and authorized the app. If this is true, then we make a request to our `getUserInfo` factory function and store the response in the user scope object. You can log the response to make sure that the logged-in user's data is being returned in the response.

Next, we will create a directive to show the welcome message to the user and provide links for logout and also a button to trigger the Facebook login.

Let's create a directive called `facebookCheck` in the `directives.js` file as follows:

```
.directive('facebookCheck', ['Facebook',
    function(Facebook) {

        return {
            link: function(scope, elements, attrs) {

                scope.login = function() {

                    Facebook.login();
                };
                scope.logout = function() {
                    Facebook.logout();
                };
            },

            templateUrl: 'partials/facebook-check.html'
        };
    }
]);
```

Next, we create our template for this directive. Please create a file called `facebook-check.html` in the `partials` folder with the following piece of code:

```
<div class='greeting'>
<p ng-if="user.name"> Welcome {{user.name}} |<a href="#/add"> Add
Products</a> |<a href class="glyphicon glyphicon-off" ng-
click="logout()"></a></p>
<button class="btn-small btn-info" ng-if="!user.name" ng-
click="login()"> FB Login</button>
</div>
```

We use `ng-if` to check if `user.name` is present. If yes, we display the **Welcome** message, and if not, we will show the Facebook login button.

The last step is to add the directive to our `index.html` file. We will add it within the `<nav>` element as follows:

```
<nav>
......
<div class= "col-md-4 pull-right" facebook-check>
</div>
</nav>
```

Save your files, and test your Facebook login to ensure that it is working. For the sake of better aesthetics, go ahead and add the following CSS class in your `app.css` to ensure that your welcome text is lined up and is in white color:

```css
.greeting, .greeting a{
  color:#fff;
  line-height: 30px;
}
```

Integrating AWS JS SDK with our application

Now, we will integrate the AWS services with our application. Amazon has released a client-side SDK called AWS JS SDK. You can read more about it at `http://aws.amazon.com/sdkforbrowser/`.

We will be using this SDK to interact with our S3 bucket and DynamoDB table. We start by including the JS SDK file in our `index.html` file as follows:

```html
<script src="https://sdk.amazonaws.com/js/aws-sdk-2.0.0-rc.17.min.js"></script>
```

Next, we will create our provider service, which will contain all of the methods required for us to interact with the AWS SDK.

Creating the AWS service provider

The provider is a core type of recipe, and all other types such as factories and services are derived from the provider. The provider allows us to create additional methods that can be used to configure it.

Let's create our provider in our `app/js/services.js` file as follows:

```javascript
.provider('AWSservice', [
      function() {

            var region, S3bucketName, dynamoTableName, roleArn,
dynamo, s3bucket;

            this.setRoleArn = function(arn) {
                roleArn = arn;
```

```
        };
        this.setRegion = function(myRegion) {
            region = myRegion;

        };
        this.setS3Bucket = function(s3) {
            S3bucketName = s3;

        };
        this.setDynamoTableName = function(dynamo) {
            dynamoTableName = dynamo;

        };
        this.$get = function($q,$log) {
            return {
            };
        };
    };
}]);
```

We call our provider AWSservice and start by declaring a couple of variables that we will need. Next, we define the methods that we will use to set the configuration parameters needed to authenticate with AWS. We will also define the methods that are needed to carry out the various operations with DynamoDB and S3.

The $get function is a factory function and works just like the factory recipe we have seen so far.

We will set these parameters in our app/app.js file as a config function as follows:

```
.config(['AWSserviceProvider',function(AWSserviceProvider){
    AWSserviceProvider.setRoleArn('<arn name>');
    AWSserviceProvider.setRegion('<AWS region name>');
    AWSserviceProvider.setS3Bucket('<S3 bucket name>');
    AWSserviceProvider.setDynamoTableName('<dynamo table name>');

}]);
```

Now, within the return part of our $get factory function, we will create our AWS initialization function as follows:

```
initializeAWS: function(token) {
    var d = $q.defer();

    var AWSCredentials = {
        RoleArn: roleArn,
```

```
            ProviderId: 'graph.facebook.com',
            WebIdentityToken: token
    };

    AWS.config.credentials = new AWS.WebIdentityCredentials(AWSCreden
tials);
    d.resolve(AWS.config.credentials);
    AWS.config.region = region;

    dynamo = new AWS.DynamoDB({
        params: {
            TableName: dynamoTableName
        }
    });
    s3bucket = new AWS.S3({
        params: {
            Bucket: S3bucketName
        }
    });

    return d.promise;

},
```

As you can see, our `initializeAWS` function accepts an argument called `token`; this will be the access token that we receive from our identity provider after a successful authentication from Facebook. We use this token along with `roleArn` as credentials to the AWS config function.

Next, we create our `dynamo` and `S3bucket` objects, which we will need later in this chapter. Also note that we are making use of the promise to ensure that we get back a response for AWS after a successful authentication.

Next, we will call our `initializeAWS` function from within our `AppCtrl` controller as highlighted.

```
Facebook.getLoginStatus(function(response) {

    if (response.status == 'connected') {
        //get logged in User info
        authService.getUserInfo().then(function(data) {
            $scope.user = data;

        })
```

```
    //Initialize AWS
    var token = response.authResponse.accessToken;

    AWSservice.initializeAWS(token).then(
        function(data) {
            $log.info(data)
        })

} else {
    Facebook.login();
}

});
```

Don't forget to add `AWSservice` and `$log` as dependencies to the `AppCtrl` controller. Run the application on the browser, and check the console to see the response from AWS.

Building our Add Products page

Now that we have Facebook authentication and the AWS SDK set up, we'll start working on the page to allow users to upload their products for sale.

We start by building our method that will insert the data into the DynamoDB table.

Saving data in DynamoDB tables

Within our AWSservice provider, we will create our new function to save the product data as follows:

```
saveProductData: function(newProduct) {

    var timestamp = new Date().getTime();
    var UUID = newProduct.userId + "-" + timestamp;
    var productData = {
        Item: {
            'product_id': {S: UUID },
            'category': { S: newProduct.category },
            'title': { S: newProduct.title},
            'description': {S: newProduct.description},
            'price': {N: newProduct.price.toString()},
            'productPicUrl': {S: newProduct.picUrl},
```

```
            'userId': {S: newProduct.userId},
            'userName': { S: newProduct.userName}

        }

    };

    dynamo.putItem(productData, function(err) {

        if (err) {
            $log.error(err);
        } else {
            $log.info('Product Saved!!');
        }
    });

},
```

Our `saveProductData` function will accept an object as an input parameter. The next piece of code is essentially to generate a sort of **Universally Unique Identifier (UUID)** by concatenating `userid` and `timestamp`.

Next, we create our `ProductData` object in the format that `DynamoDB` can understand. As you can see, while passing each attribute field, we also need to define the data type for that attribute. The notation `S` stands for string and `N` stands for number.

The last piece of code calls the `putItem` method that will save this data in our DynamoDB table.

Creating the view for the add product form

To build out the view, create a file called `add-products.html` in the `partials` folder with the following code:

```
<h1>Add your Product</h1>
<hr/>

<form role="form" id="add-page" ng-submit="addProduct()">

    <div class="form-group">
        <label>Category</label>
        <select ng-model="newProduct.category">
            <option ng-repeat="category in categories">{{category}}</
option>
```

```
            </select>
        </div>

        <div class="form-group">
            <label>Product Title</label>
            <input class="form-control" type="text" ng-model="newProduct.
title" />
        </div>

        <div class="form-group">
            <label>Product Description</label>
            <textarea rows="8" class="form-control" type="text" ng-
model="newProduct.description"></textarea>
        </div>

        <div class="form-group">
            <label>Product Price</label>
            <input class="form-control" type="number" ng-
model="newProduct.price">
        </div>

        <div>
            <input type="submit" class="btn btn-success" value="List My
Product">
        </div>

    </form>
```

This is a regular form with fields to select a category, add a title, description, and price.

Building the controller for the add products view

Let's create a controller called AddProductsCtrl in our controllers.js file, and add the following piece of code to it:

```
.controller('AddProductsCtrl', ['$scope', 'categoryService',
'authService', 'AWSservice',
    function($scope, categoryService, authService, AWSservice) {

        $scope.categories = categoryService.getCategories();

        $scope.newProduct = {};
```

```
$scope.addProduct = function() {

        $scope.newProduct.userId = $scope.user.id;
        $scope.newProduct.userName = $scope.user.name;
        $scope.newProduct.picUrl = 'sw3/someURL';
AWSservice.saveProductData($scope.newProduct);

    }

    }
]);
```

The controller code is quite straightforward. We first populate the categories scope by calling the getCategoriesMethod of the categoriesService. Next, we capture some additional information such as the logged-in user's ID and name, and push them into the newProduct object along with the other data that is coming in from the form.

You'll also notice that we have a property called picUrl, where, for the time being, we are passing in a dummy value; we will change this once we get to our next section on uploading images.

This should be good for now. Save the files, and in the browser, navigate to http://localhost:8000/app/#/add and test out adding a couple of products.

You should receive a **Product Saved** message in your console on successful execution. Head over to the AWS management console, and verify that the data is saved in your DynamoDB table.

Uploading images to S3

Now, we'll see how to upload the product pictures along with our add product form. We'll start by adding the markup for file upload in the add-products.html partial:

```
<img width="250" ng-src="{{uploadedPicURL}}">
<div class="form-group">
<label>Product Picture</label>
<input class="form-control" type="file" accept="image/*" ng-
  model="newProduct.pic" onchange="angular.element(this).scope().
uploadImage(this.files)">
</div>
```

Our intention is to start the file upload on to S3 as soon as a file is selected; hence, we use the `onchange` event. Again, from a usability standpoint, it makes sense to keep this piece of code at the top (preferably, after the category select box) so that after selecting the file, as the user is filling up the rest of the form, the image would have already been uploaded into S3, assuming that the file being uploaded is not very large in size.

We also have an `img` tag that will show the preview of the uploaded picture. Next, we will write our `uploadImage` method within the `AddProductsCtrl` controller:

```
$scope.uploadImage = function(files) {
    AWSservice.uploadPic(files).then(
        function(data) {

            $scope.newProduct.picUrl = data;
            $scope.uploadedPicURL = "https://s3.amazonaws.com/garage-
                commerce/" + data;
        }, function(err) {
            $log.error(err);
        })
}
```

The controller is quite simple; it takes the `files` object as an input argument and passes it to the factory function, waits for the promise to resolve, and sets the filename and image path in the scope properties. You would ideally want to store the `S3bucket` name in a scope property and use it to dynamically build the `uploadedPic` URL.

 Don't forget to remove the dummy picURL value that we were passing earlier in the `addProduct` method.

Next, we will work on the crucial piece, the factory service function that will do the job of uploading that file into S3.

We are going to create our function called `uploadPic` within the `AWSservice` factory and put in this following piece of code:

```
uploadPic: function(files) {
    var d = $q.defer();
    var file = files[0];
    var data = {
        Key: file.name,
        Body: file,
        ContentType: file.type
    };
```

```
s3bucket.putObject(data, function(err, data) {
    var fileName = file.name;
    d.resolve(fileName);

    if (err) {
        d.reject(err);
        $log.error(err);
    } else {
        $log.info('successfully uploaded');
    }
});
return d.promise;
},
```

We first create an instance of our S3 object; then, we capture the file data in a data object. Using the `s3.putObject` method, we upload the data into S3. As we do not know how much time it would take for the file to upload, we set up a promise so that we get the callback once the file is successfully uploaded.

 To keep things simple, we are uploading the image with the original filename. However, for a production-level setup, you might want to rename the files with some kind of a UUID to avoid overwrites.

Test out the add products form, and make sure that the images are getting uploaded on S3 and the data is being saved in the database. Go ahead and add a couple of products by selecting different categories.

Fetching the products lists for a category

The next step is to work on our product listing pages. The idea is when the user selects a category from the navigation bar, we show them the list of products belonging to that category.

DynamoDB provides two methods to fetch a group of listing:

- **Scan**: This operation runs through every record in the database and returns a result set that matches the comparison parameters
- **Query**: This operation, on the other hand, will find items or rows only using the primary key values; they can be hash key or range key values

Both query and scan operations return a maximum of 1 MB of data. In our case, we will use the scan operation along with `ScanFilter` to get the matching records for a given category.

We'll head to our `AWSservice` factory and create a function called `getProductsByCategory` with the following code:

```
getProductsByCategory: function(category) {
    var d = $q.defer();
    var params = {
        'Limit': 100,
        'ScanFilter': {
            category: {
                AttributeValueList: [{
                    S: category
                }],
                ComparisonOperator: 'EQ'
            }
        }
    };
    dynamo.scan(params, function(err, data) {
        if (data) {
            d.resolve(data);
        } else if (err) {
            $log.error(err);
        }
    });
    return d.promise;
},
```

The piece of code that is interesting to look at is the formation of the `params` object, where we are setting up `ScanFilter`. The syntax of `ScanFilter` isn't quite straightforward as you might have seen earlier.

We need to pass `attributeName` or field name on which you want to set the filter, then we pass the attribute's value that we need to compare, and finally, we set the comparison operator. As we need to show results for the selected category, we use the EQ operator. The other operators that the `ComparisionOperator` accepts are as follows:

- NE | LE | LT | GE | GT | NOT_NULL | NULL | CONTAINS | NOT_CONTAINS | BEGINS_WITH | IN | BETWEEN

Now, we'll get to call our factory function, within the `ProductsCtrl` controller:

```
AWSservice.getProductsByCategory($scope.category).then(
    function(data) {
        $scope.productsListing = data.Items;
    })
```

Save the file, and refresh your page. You may get an error that says **No credentials to load** or something to that effect on the developer console. Ignore it for now. Wait for a few seconds, and try clicking on any of the other categories from the navigation bar. You should get to see the products getting displayed with funny extensions such as `.S` and `.N` appended to the products titles and price values. We'll get to this later.

The reason why we get the **No credentials** message is because the request to the `getProductsByCategory` method gets fired before our AWS authentications and initialization takes place.

Using resolves to preload data

So, the question we have at hand is how to make sure that our Facebook authentication and AWS initialization take place before our `productsCtrl` and its methods are executed. AngularJS provides a nifty little solution called resolve, which is available as a part of both the UI-Router and ngRoute modules.

Resolve will let you execute functions and inject the resolved data into the route's controller. We can also create nested resolves and use the same method in the following example.

Let's go ahead and set up the resolve. Resolves are set within the `StateProvider`, so we will add the following code in our `app.js` file as highlighted. We will modify our category state as follows:

```
$stateProvider.state('category', {
    url: '/:category',
    templateUrl: 'partials/products.html',
    controller: 'ProductsCtrl',
    resolve: {
        Facebook: 'Facebook',
        FBtoken: function(Facebook) {

            return Facebook.getLoginStatus(function(response) {
                if (response.status == 'connected') {
                    return response.token;
                }
```

```
            })
        }
    },
});
```

Resolve takes in an object that needs to be in the form of a key-value pair. The dependencies need to be defined as a key, and the factory function that needs to be resolved is the value of the key-value pair.

The preceding FBtoken function will resolve and return the access token. We now need to create our nested resolve that will take this access token and authenticate our AWS objects. We do this in the following manner:

```
AWSinit: function(FBtoken, AWSservice) {
    var token = FBtoken.authResponse.accessToken;
    return AWSservice.initializeAWS(token).$promise;

}
```

Now, as we refactored our code to initialize our AWS objects in the resolve, we no longer need to do it again from within our AppCtrlm. So, go ahead and remove the AWSservice.initializeAWS call from within the AppCtrl controller function.

Save the files, hit one of the categories URL, and ensure that the products are showing up without any errors on the console. Next, we'll get rid of the additional s and n notations that get added to the end of the titles and price.

If you log the response of the getProductsByCategory method, you'll notice that AWS is adding these s and n notations to the values to denote strings or numbers. To get rid of these is quite simple. We'll simply modify our products.html partial to append these values to our expressions as follows:

```
<h2><a href="#/{{category +'/'+product.product_id.S}}">{{product.
title.S}}</a> </h2>
<h5>{{product.price.N |currency}}</h5>
<p><i>-by:{{product.userName.S}}</i></p>
```

Creating our product details page

Next, we will build our product details page. We'll try this by writing out the factory service that will return the data for the selected product. Within the AWSservice provider, create the following function:

```
getProductDetails: function(id) {
    var d = $q.defer();
```

```
        var params = {
            'Key': {'product_id': {'S': id}
            }
        };
        dynamo.getItem(params, function(err, data) {
            if (err) $log.error('err= ' + err);
            if (data) {
                d.resolve(data);
            }
        });
        return d.promise;
    },
```

The code will look familiar to you by now. We build the params object with the key parameter. Note that the key parameter always needs to be the hash value. In case you defined a RangeKey while creating your table, you will also need to set the RangeKey values while building the params object.

Once the object is ready, we pass it to the getItem method and wait to hear from DynamoDB.

Next, we'll replace the static data with the actual code within the ProductDetailsCtrl controller as follows:

```
.controller('ProductDetailsCtrl', ['$scope', '$stateParams',
'AWSservice', '$log',
    function($scope, $stateParams, AWSservice, $log) {
        var id = $stateParams.id;
        AWSservice.getProductDetails(id).then(
            function(data) {
                $scope.product = data.Item;
            }, function(err) {
                $log.error(err);
            });
    }
])
```

Now, we'll create the partial view that will display the product info. Let's edit the file called product-details.html with the following short piece of code:

```
<h1>{{product.title.S}}</h1>
<img ng-src="https://s3.amazonaws.com/garage-commerce/{{product.
productPicUrl.S}}">
<p>{{product.description.S}}</p>
<h3>{{product.price.N|currency}}</h3>
```

Adding products to cart

So, now that we have our product details page ready, we will build the **Add to Cart** functionality.

Let's add the **Add to Cart** button on the `product.details.html` page as follows:

```
<button class="btn btn-success" ng-
click="addToCart(product.product_id.S)">Add to Cart</button>
```

Next, let's add the controller function within the `ProductDetailsCtrl` controller:

```
$scope.addToCart=function(product_id){
$scope.shoppingBasket.push(product_id);
}
```

For now, we are pushing the product IDs into an AngularJS scope. Alternatively, you would want to save this information in another DynamoDB. This will allow you to build further on features such as abandoned carts and also not let you lose out on the scope values each time you refresh the page.

The checkout page

Now that items are getting added to the cart, let's work on the checkout page. We start by adding this new state in `stateProvider` in the `app.js` file as follows:

```
$stateProvider.state('checkout', {
    url:'/checkout',
    templateUrl: 'partials/checkout.html',
    controller: 'CheckoutCtrl'
});
```

Make sure that this is your first state in the list of routes or at least above the category state route. If not, AngularJS will treat `/checkout` as another category.

The controller for our checkout page would look like this:

```
.controller('CheckoutCtrl', ['$scope', 'AWSservice',
    function($scope, AWSservice) {
        $scope.totalPrice = 0;
        $scope.checkoutList = [];
        angular.forEach($scope.shoppingBasket, function(item) {
            AWSservice.getProductDetails(item).then(
                function(data) {
```

```
                    var basketItem = {};
                    basketItem.title = data.Item.title.S;
                    basketItem.price = data.Item.price.N;
                    $scope.totalPrice = $scope.totalPrice +
                        parseInt(basketItem.price);
                    $scope.checkoutList.push(basketItem);
                }, function(err) {
                    $log.error(err);
                }
            );
        });
    }
])
```

We iterate through each item from our `shoppingBasket` scope object and fire a request to our `getProductDetails` function to get the details of the product. We then push the title and price into an array, which we'll call `checkoutList`.

We'll now create the partial called `checkout.html` with the following code:

```html
<h1>Checkout</h1>
<hr/>

<div class="col-md-10">
    <table class="table">
        <thead>
            <tr>
                <th>No.</th>
                <th>Product</th>
                <th>Price</th>
            </tr>
        </thead>
        <tbody>
            <tr ng-repeat="item in checkoutList">
                <td>{{$index+1}}</td>
                <td>{{item.title}}</td>
                <td>{{item.price|currency}}</td>
            </tr>
            <tr>
                <td></td>
                <td>
                    <strong>Total</strong>
                </td>
                <td>
```

```
                    <strong>{{totalPrice|currency}}</strong>
                </td>
            </tr>
        </tbody>
    </table>
</div>
```

The code for the partial simply runs an `ng-repeat` directive to list out all the items in the `checkoutList` array.

Let's also add the `View Shopping Basket` link in our `index.html` file as highlighted:

```
<a class=" col-md-2 pull-right" href="#/checkout">View Shopping Basket
</a>
    <div ui-view></div>
```

Saving the orders

The final step would be to save the order details into another table. Let's create a table on DynamoDB, call it `garage-commerce-orders`, and set the primary hash key as `order_id`.

Let's add our checkout button to our `checkout.html` partial:

```
<div class="col-md-1 pull-right">
    <button class="btn btn-success" ng-click="placeOrder()"> Place
Order</button>
</div>
```

The controller function for this within the `checkoutCtrl` would look like this:

```
$scope.placeOrder=function(){
    AWSservice.saveOrder($scope.checkoutList,$scope.user.id);
};
```

Finally, the `saveOrder` function service in the `AWSservice` provider will look like this:

```
saveOrder: function(orders, buyer_id) {
    var orderString = JSON.stringify(orders);
    AWS.config.region = region;
    var timestamp = new Date().getTime();
    var UUID = "#" + buyer_id + "-" + timestamp;

    var dynamo = new AWS.DynamoDB({
```

```
        params: {TableName: 'garage-commerce-orders'}
    });
    var orderData = {
        Item:
        {'order_id': {S:UUID},
        'buyer_id': {S:buyer_id},
        'order_data':{S: orderString}
        }

    };

    dynamo.putItem(orderData, function(err, data) {
        if (err) $log.error(err);

    });

}
```

With this, we complete our Garage Commerce app. Refresh your browsers, and play around and enjoy.

Summary

Building a full-fledged e-commerce site is a fairly large exercise. In this chapter, the idea was to get you comfortable with the various tools and services involved and lay the groundwork for you to go ahead and build on top of it.

In this chapter, we saw:

- How to go about using the AWS services, namely S3 and DynamoDB. We took advantage of the AWS JS SDK to interact with these services and store data in them.

- We saw how to integrate Facebook and use it with Amazon's Web Identity Federation to authenticate access to the AWS services.

- We stored and retrieved data from databases and uploaded files into S3 using pure JavaScript, which I'm sure is a delight for many frontend developers.

- We saw the problems related to asynchronous calls and saw how to use resolve to ensure that data is preloaded before the route controller function is called.

Like always, there is so much more you can do to further enhance and improve the app that you've built. In case you are looking to build on this further, here are a couple of things you can try adding:

- A payment gateway so that customers can make payments using their credit card. For PayPal, have a look at its Adaptive Payments API at `https://developer.paypal.com/docs/classic/adaptive-payments/gs_AdaptivePayments/`.

- You can also look at `stripe.com` as a payment option.

- Build out an admin section that allows you to see all the orders and abandoned carts in the system. These would be simple functions that read data out from the DynamoDB database.

- Try adding a keyword search using AngularJS filters.

I hope you enjoyed building your very own e-commerce app.

AngularJS Resources

AngularJS is amongst the most popular JS MVC frameworks. An active community supports it and is constantly helping it to grow.

The following resources will help you in your journey with AngularJS.

Official resources

The following are some of the official resources that will help you:

- **AngularJS** (the official site): https://angularjs.org/
- **GitHub** (the GitHub repository): https://github.com/angular/angular.js
- **YouTube**: https://www.youtube.com/user/angularjs
- **Twitter**: https://twitter.com/angularjs

Recommended AngularJS modules

- **AngularUI**: http://angular-ui.github.io/
  Officially managed collection of commonly-used modules.

- **ngModules.org**: http://ngmodules.org/
  Searchable repository of all AngularJS modules.

Boiler plates

- **Angular Seed**: https://github.com/angular/angular-seed
- **ngBoilerplate**: https://github.com/ngbp/ngbp
- **Yeoman**: http://yeoman.io/

Learning resources

- **AngularJS in 60ish Minutes**: `https://www.youtube.com/watch?v=i9MHigUZKEM`

  The first thing to watch when starting with AngularJS.

- **AngularJS Learning**: `https://github.com/jmcunningham/AngularJS-Learning`

  An exhaustive collection of links to various resources.

- **AngularJS Lessons**: `https://egghead.io/technologies/angularjs`

  Good and extensive collection of quick short videos on the basics and advanced features of AngularJS.

- **stackoverflow**: `http://stackoverflow.com/questions/tagged/angularjs`

  If you encounter any problems, there are chances that someone has already answered the same question here.

- **AngularJS Google Groups**: `https://groups.google.com/forum/#!forum/angular`

  Place where most of the AngularJS core group members and other smart people hang out and reply to questions.

- **AngularJS IRC Chat Group**: `http://webchat.freenode.net/?channels=angularjs&uio=d4`

  Immediate answers to your questions, in case you didn't find them in the earlier two places.

Good friends with AngularJS (third-party tools and services)

- **Iconic Framework**: `http://ionicframework.com/`

  A great framework to build Hybrid mobile apps with Angular.

- **Firebase**: `https://www.firebase.com/`

  The perfect tool for storing data and also provides real-time sync to all connected devices.

- **famo.us**: `https://famo.us`

  The newly launched JS framework for building rich interactive UIs now supports integration with Angular to manage data.

Core team members and knowledgeable people to follow

- **Miško Hevery**: `http://misko.hevery.com/about/`

  The 'Father' of AngularJS.

- **Brad Green**: `https://twitter.com/bradlygreen`

  He is the Project Manager at AngularJS. He has written a book on the technology and tweets interesting news based on Angular.

- **Igor Minar**: `https://github.com/IgorMinar`

  He is one of the core group members and has a very good collection of GitHub repositories of apps built on Angular.

- **Vojta Jina**: `https://github.com/vojtajina`

  He is another core group member who has worked extensively on Unit Testing frameworks for Angular.

- **James deBoer**: `https://plus.google.com/116361169772404573567/posts`

  He is part of the core team that works on AngularDart.

- **Dan Wahlin**: `https://twitter.com/DanWahlin`

  He is a strong proponent of Angular JS, who has worked on numerous tutorials and blogs, and has been conducting training sessions on AngularJS and other frontend technologies.

- **Caitlin Potter**: `https://twitter.com/caitp88`

  She is an active contributor to the AngularJS project.

- **Pete Bacon Darwin**: `https://twitter.com/petebd`

  He helps people to solve their problems in AngularJS.

Index

A

Thank you for buying
AngularJS Web Application
Development Blueprints

About Packt Publishing

Packt, pronounced 'packed', published its first book "*Mastering phpMyAdmin for Effective MySQL Management*" in April 2004 and subsequently continued to specialize in publishing highly focused books on specific technologies and solutions.

Our books and publications share the experiences of your fellow IT professionals in adapting and customizing today's systems, applications, and frameworks. Our solution based books give you the knowledge and power to customize the software and technologies you're using to get the job done. Packt books are more specific and less general than the IT books you have seen in the past. Our unique business model allows us to bring you more focused information, giving you more of what you need to know, and less of what you don't.

Packt is a modern, yet unique publishing company, which focuses on producing quality, cutting-edge books for communities of developers, administrators, and newbies alike. For more information, please visit our website: www.packtpub.com.

About Packt Open Source

In 2010, Packt launched two new brands, Packt Open Source and Packt Enterprise, in order to continue its focus on specialization. This book is part of the Packt Open Source brand, home to books published on software built around Open Source licenses, and offering information to anybody from advanced developers to budding web designers. The Open Source brand also runs Packt's Open Source Royalty Scheme, by which Packt gives a royalty to each Open Source project about whose software a book is sold.

Writing for Packt

We welcome all inquiries from people who are interested in authoring. Book proposals should be sent to author@packtpub.com. If your book idea is still at an early stage and you would like to discuss it first before writing a formal book proposal, contact us; one of our commissioning editors will get in touch with you.

We're not just looking for published authors; if you have strong technical skills but no writing experience, our experienced editors can help you develop a writing career, or simply get some additional reward for your expertise.

AngularJS Directives

ISBN: 978-1-78328-033-9   Paperback: 110 pages

Learn how to craft dynamic directives to fuel your single-page web applications using AngularJS

1. Learn how to build an AngularJS directive.

2. Create extendable modules for plug-and-play usability.

3. Build apps that react in real time to changes in your data model.

Mastering Web Application Development with AngularJS

ISBN: 978-1-78216-182-0   Paperback: 372 pages

Build single-page web applications using the power of AngularJS

1. Make the most out of AngularJS by understanding the AngularJS philosophy and applying it to real-life development tasks.

2. Effectively structure, write, test, and finally deploy your application.

3. Add security and optimization features to your AngularJS applications.

Please check **www.PacktPub.com** for information on our titles

Instant AngularJS Starter

ISBN: 978-1-78216-676-4   Paperback: 66 pages

A concise guide to start building dynamic web applications with AngularJS, one of the Web's most innovative JavaScript frameworks

1. Learn something new in an Instant! A short, fast, focused guide delivering immediate results.

2. Take a broad look at the capabilities of AngularJS, with in-depth analysis of its key features.

3. See how to build a structured MVC-style application that will scale gracefully in real-world applications.

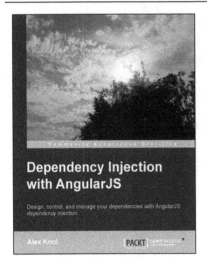

Dependency Injection with AngularJS

ISBN: 978-1-78216-656-6   Paperback: 78 pages

Design, control, and manage your dependencies with AngularJS dependency injection

1. Understand the concept of dependency injection.

2. Isolate units of code during testing JavaScript using Jasmine.

3. Create reusable components in AngularJS.

www.ingramcontent.com/pod-product-compliance
Lightning Source LLC
Chambersburg PA
CBHW060516060326
40690CB00017B/3296